The Jewish Community
of Rouyn–Noranda

The
Jewish Community
of
Rouyn–Noranda

The life and history of a small
Jewish community in Northern Quebec
(remembered by those who lived there)

ISBN 978-1-989255-03-2

Book Committee: Rosalie (Mednick) Nepom, Sol Mednick,
Harvey Korman, Esther (Korman) Verred, Dr. Isaac Katz
Editor & Designer: Bill Gladstone

Table of Contents

Acknowledgements

MY ORIGINAL THOUGHT for this book was to tell a story that presented the growth, pains and innermost feelings of the Jews who established themselves and their families in the twin cities of Rouyn–Noranda.

When I asked my brother Sol to help me he did, bringing his huge energy and interest, and as a result, this book just grew and grew.

In addition we were blessed to have the tireless working committee of Dr. Isaac Katz, Harvey Korman and Esther (Korman) Verred. This group worked endlessly and for this they deserve our many thanks and much appreciation.

Their vigour and dedication have helped make this book complete and compelling. And many many thanks to our amazing editor, Bill Gladstone, for his insight and guidance throughout.

Our sincerest gratitude and appreciation to all who helped make *The Jewish Community of Rouyn–Noranda* a book filled with poignant memories for present and for future generations. §

Envisioned and conceived by:
Rosalie (Mednick) Nepom
Sol Mednick
Toronto, Spring 2023

Preface

WE WOULD LIKE TO DEDICATE this book to all the small Jewish communities that were established in northern Quebec and northern Ontario.

We remember growing up in one such community, Rouyn–Noranda in northern Quebec. A mining town, its main landmarks were the ever-present towering double smokestacks of Noranda Mines. And its most unforgettable feature was undoubtedly the biting cold of winter and the forbidding landscape of snow and ice it produced.

As history tells us, the nineteenth century was a difficult time for the Jewish population of Eastern Europe and the Pale of Settlement, the western provinces of Russia where Jews were permitted to live. In 1881, the Russian Czar Alexander II was assassinated. As usual, the Jews were blamed and severe pogroms erupted throughout the Russian Empire. Jewish homes, businesses, shuls and institutions were attacked and destroyed. Thousands were murdered and severely injured.

The early twentieth century saw the renewal of another wave

of pogroms, beginning with the devastating Kishinev (Chisinau) pogrom in 1905, sparking a new stream of Jewish refugees. The United States was the most desirable destination, and eventually more than two million Jews reached America. Then, in 1924, the United States Congress passed a law which excluded Eastern Europe Jews and others from immigrating to America; the number of admissable refugees decreased from approximately 100,000 to only 10,000 annually.

Canada was still accepting large numbers of Jews until the Liberal Government of Mackenzie King, with its "none is too many" policy, brought Jewish immigration almost to a complete halt.

PROSPECTORS in the early 1920s discovered copper and gold deposits in the area around Rouyn, sparking an epic mining rush. That attracted a number of Jewish business people who recognized the beneficient opportunities available in Rouyn and its newly-born twin, Noranda, where the English-speaking newcomers and many of the Jewish families tended to gravitate. Rouyn and Noranda quickly came to life in the boreal forest, becoming populous and organized communities. Photos of the late 1920s show a rugged pioneer town with mud streets and lots of wood-frame buildings.

It is a matter of debate as to who was the first Jewish settler in the towns. By one account Louis Scott, a businessman involved in real estate, road construction and the timber trade, can claim the honour. "Although there was undoubtedly some Jewish travelers who came here from the earliest days, the first to settle in the fall of 1924 and to guide with the other pioneers in the formative period of the district, was Louis Scott," noted historian Albert Leury (translated from French).

But according to the description of the new synagogue's dedication ceremony in October 1949, the Rouyn–Noranda Press asserted that "Mr. and Mrs. D[avid] Caplan were the first Jewish people to come to the twin cities, and that they were followed by Mr.

Noranda, Que.—Jewish ·ngrega-
tion of Noranda, 2.00; R. Mendel
Katz, 10.00; A. J. Korman 2.00; J.
Korman, 3.00; J. Mednick 1.00; S.
Sandberg, 1.00; H. Taitle um, .50.
Rouyn, Que.—D. Caplan 1.00; S.
Kravitz, 1.00.

This list of donors from Rouyn–Noranda to the United Jewish Philanthropic Fund was published in the Canadian Jewish Review for its Rosh Hashanah edition in 1932. Donors included Rev. Mendel Katz, A. J. Korman, J. Korman, J. Mednick, S. Sandberg, H. Taitlebaum, D. Caplan and S. Kravitz.

and Mrs. I[saac] Rice, Mr. and Mrs. Louis Scott, Mr. and Mrs. Sidney Sandberg and Mr. and Mrs. Mike Korman." Some of these people, particularly David Caplan and Isaac Rice, contributed significantly to the construction of Rouyn in its early years.

There were about a dozen Jewish families in the twin towns by the end of 1927, and about twenty local families in 1932 when the first synagogue opened. By then the town's esteemed religious leader, Rabbi Mendel Katz, had arrived. Soon prosperous local merchants such as Joseph Korman and Joseph Mednick would build numerous local commercial and residential properties. And Sam Bucovetsky of Timmins would open two department stores, part of his chain of northern stores, and David Korman of Englehart would build the Capitol Theatre (English) and Paramount Theatre (French) in Rouyn and the Noranda Theatre (English) in Noranda.

Members of the Jewish community, including our parents and grandparents, were mostly recent immigrants who came seeking a safe place to earn their livings, raise their families and maintain their Yiddishkeit. They worked in diverse fields of commercial and professional activity: clothing, tailoring, jewelry, furniture, theatre, electricity, produce, meats, groceries, beer, dairy, pharmacy, dyeing, law and dentistry.

The 1930s, 1940s and 1950s were the community's heydays. The children thrived within Rouyn–Noranda's excellent schooling system, resulting in a generation of achievers who went on to lead productive and meaningful lives.

The Jewish population of Rouyn–Noranda was always in flux, but the community began to trickle away in the 1950s, a net deficit that gained momentum in the 1960s. By the 1970s the community was just a shell of its former self. Many of the town's non-Jewish English speakers also left. In 1973, around the time of the Yom Kippur War, community elders sold the synagogue to the Lion's Club for $35,000 and donated the proceeds to Israel.

Fifty years after this definitive act of closure, we still remember our birthplace with pride and affection. The town produced a generation of hardy souls who went on to strengthen the fabric of the larger communities of Montreal, Toronto, Winnipeg, Halifax and many smaller cities. We witnessed the Jewish community of Rouyn–Noranda as it developed and thrived vibrantly. Then we saw it pass on into history, as all things must. §

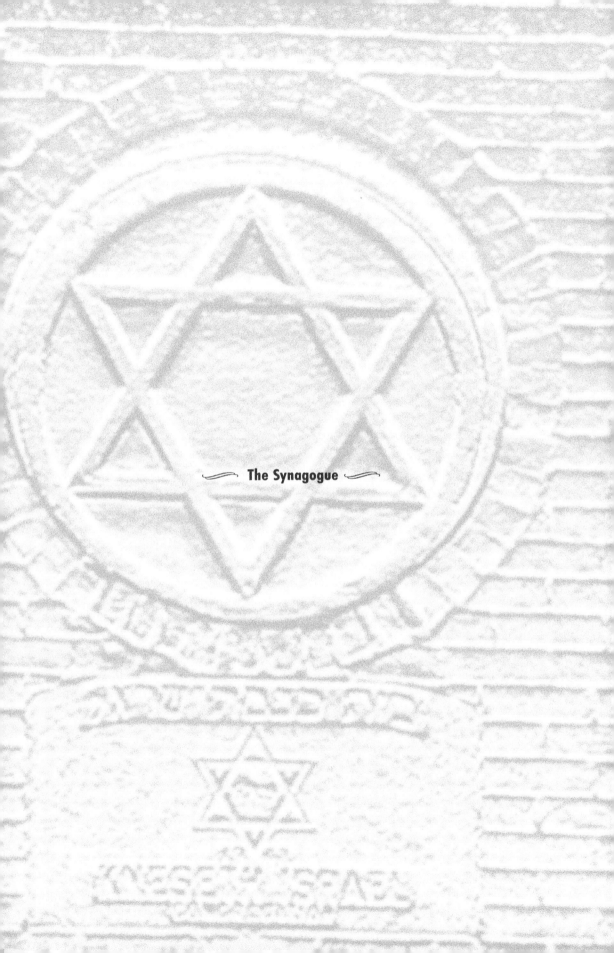

The Synagogue

ROUYN-NORANDA PRESS
P. C., OCT. 27/49

New Synagogue Officially Opened Following Parade Last Sunday

Michael Korman, president of the local Jewish Community, cut the ribbon to officially open the New Kneseth Israel Synagogue on Ninth Street in Noranda last Sunday afternoon. The short opening ceremony followed a parade of the Jewish Community led by the Canadian Corps Band from the home of Joseph Korman on Third Avenue.

Joseph Korman cut the ribbon on the inner door to open the main part of the building. In the procession Mr. Korman carried the scrolls of the Torah which he and Mrs. Korman and their son had presented to the synagogue. A religious service was held commemorating the official opening.

A dinner and dance was held in the hall in the evening to mark the happy occasion for the local Jewish community. Dr. Harry Ironstone presided at the dinner and welcomed the out of town guests. In his opening remarks he recalled that Mr. and Mrs. D. Caplan were the first Jewish people to come to the twin cities, and that they were followed by Mr. and Mrs. I. Rice, Mr. and Mrs. Louis Scott, Mr. and Mrs. Sidney Sandberg and Mr. and Mrs. Mike Korman.

Praise was given to the work of Michael Korman who had given so much of his time to see that the new building was built. He was presented following the dinner with a gold watch by Nathan Weisenthal on behalf of the Jewish community. Wallets were also presented to B. Zifkin and Charles Steinberg in appreciation of their work.

Among the speakers were Joseph Korman, I. Rice, of the building committee, Mrs. Louis Scott, president of the Ladies Hadassah; Louis Revzen, president of B'Nai B'rith; Sam Davis, Kirkland Lake, Jack Ritter, M. Sharony, Frank Conlon, editor of the Rouyn-Noranda Press; and others.

Following the dinner dancing was enjoyed to the music of Harry Byzick and his orchestra.

The "new" Beit Kneseth Israel Synagogue, completed in 1948 and dedicated in 1949, was the main social hub of the community for more than two decades, and replaced an earlier synagogue on the site. After its sale in 1972, it was converted into an apartment building.

A Brief History of Kneseth Israel Synagogue
by Dr Isaac Katz

THE JEWISH COMMUNITY of Rouyn–Noranda evolved with people like our parents and grandparents who settled there to start a new life in a safe and secure environment. The first Jewish families arrived in around 1924–1925 when the railroad was extended into that area. They came with other European immigrants from other parts of Canada who were looking for work and opportunity. The mining and forestry industries were quite active and people were able to settle down, earn their living and raise their families.

The Horne Mine, later named the Noranda Mine, was discovered in 1926. It was developed in 1927 and by 1932 Rouyn–

Noranda's original Beit Kneseth Israel Synagogue, visible in the middle, was built in 1932. The wood-frame building, which stood on 9th Street, had three main windows and a distinctive Star of David above the door. This photo dates from the middle 1930s. (BANQ)

Noranda was a busy mining town. The Depression had dampened the general economy but the mining industry was not impacted to the same extent. People came to seek employment, to set up as merchants, or join the service industry. The community grew as the newcomers established retail stores, grocery stores, pharmacies, movie theatres and photo shops.

Rabbi Katz arrived in 1930 and took charge of the religious life of the community. The first synagogue, a wooden structure, was built at 18 – 9th Street in Noranda in 1932. It was replaced with a brick and stucco building in 1948 at the same location. The facade of the new synagogue was designed to represent a menorah: four windows on each side of the front door and a star of David window, representing the *shamas*, in the middle above the door.

A photo of the Torah ceremony in May 1948 (reproduced on page 22) shows Rabbi Katz holding the Torah with the white cover. The congregational president, Mr. Michel Korman, is standing in the middle with Mr. Sam Mednick to his right. The special occasion was to honour the creation of the State of Israel.

The new synagogue was officially dedicated in 1949.

Unfortunately, Rabbi Katz was in failing health and couldn't participate in the ceremony. The following is an extract of *The Rouyn-Noranda Press* dated October 27, 1949:

New Synagogue Officially Opened
Following Parade Last Sunday

Michel Korman, president of the local Jewish community, cut the ribbon to officially open the New Kneseth Israel Synagogue on Ninth Street in Noranda last Sunday afternoon. The short opening ceremony followed a parade of the Jewish community led by the Canadian Corps Band from the home of Joseph Korman on Third Avenue. He cut the ribbon on the inner door to open the main part of the building. In the procession, Mr. [Joseph] Korman carried the scrolls of the Torah which he and Mrs. Korman and their son had presented to the Synagogue. A dinner and dance was held in the hall in the evening to mark the occasion for the local Jewish community. Dr. Harry Ironstone presided at the dinner and welcomed the out-of-town guests.

Eventually the Jewish community diminished in number and the shul had to be closed. It was purchased by the Noranda Lions Club in 1972 and was eventually tranformed into an apartment building. The proceeds of this sale were donated to Israel in 1973. The five Torah scrolls were returned to the families that had donated them. Joe Korman's Torah ended up in Temple Anshe Sholom in Hamilton, and David Korman's Torah ended up in the Baycrest Synagogue in Toronto. Michel Korman's Torah ended up in Montreal. The whereabouts of the two remaining Torah scrolls are unknown.

In the 1990s the Quebec Government designated the facade of Noranda's former shul as a heritage site and it remains preserved to this day. §

The photo above shows the building's cornerstone being installed by Simcha Korman (left), Nachman Korman, Jack Ritter and Sonny Korman.

Memories of Kneseth Israel Congregation
by Esther (Korman) Verred

THE SHUL WAS AN INTEGRAL PART of Jewish life in Rouyn–Noranda. It was the factor that made the Jews into a community. Inside, the building was rather unremarkable and very utilitarian, nothing fancy at all. However it was the central gathering place of the Jewish community, similar to the churches of various European communities whose denizens immigrated to Rouyn–Noranda in those days. It was not only the place to pray together, but to celebrate happy occasions like weddings, cultural events and other activities.

A treasured photograph shows the unveiling of the cornerstone of the "new" synagogue. The cornerstone is located on the bottom right of the front of the building.

A memory of mine involves the outside of the building. We know that all Canadian children must have at least one experience of getting their tongue frozen to metal during the winter. Well, mine occurred when I was about four or five years old and I received my Canadian graduation by getting my tongue attached to the doorknob of the synagogue. I don't remember who rescued me, but remember screaming bloody murder until I was detached.

The Entrance

ONCE YOU ENTER the building there was a smallish entrance. To the left was the staircase going down to the basement. In front of that staircase was a cloakroom, where you could hang your coat, deposit boots and other paraphernalia. There was a half wall from the cloakroom to the central entranceway. At the far left of the cloakroom was the staircase to the upstairs balcony-room. On the right of the entranceway was a small classroom where children went to cheder. When I was very young these studies were very traditional, the way

Above left, Torah scrolls are carried into the new Kneseth Israel upon its completion in 1948. The three gentlemen holding the Torah scrolls are Sam Mednick (left), Michel Korman and Rabbi Katz. The young lady looking at the camera is Pearl Fried. The procession was also meant to celebrate the establishment of the new State of Israel; the photo at right may be another taken at the same event.

our grandparents and great-grandparents studied. We learned about the religion, customs, practices, and how to read and write biblical Hebrew. We used religious texts including the Torah. I remember Mr. Sharony teaching us the four questions for Pesach and its preamble, "*Tateh/Zaida, Ich vil dir fregn di fir kashes. Die ershteh kasha is . . . .*" ("Dad/Grandpa, I want to ask you the Four Questions. The first question is . . . .")

When I was older, our studies became more modern and we started to use regular, new textbooks to learn to speak, read and write modern Hebrew. Our older generations never learned to speak modern Hebrew (but they prayed and read in traditional Hebrew).

The Sanctuary

AT THE BACK of the entranceway were the doors that led into the sanctuary or prayer hall. When you entered, you would be struck by the size and expanse of this room with its vaulted two-storey ceiling. Both sides of the sanctuary were flanked by windows, making it a bright, airy room. There were three rows of pews with wide aisles between them.

As was customary, women and men didn't sit together. Originally, the woman's section was in the balcony, but in later years when the congregation got smaller, the women came downstairs. Women were in the left row, and men were in the middle and right row.

About halfway down the room was the *bimah,* an elevated altar with a railing, large enough to accommodate several people. It had a reading desk where the Torah and other prayer books were placed to be read by the religious leader and other members of the congregation. A cupboard underneath held books as well as the *shofars* which were blown on Rosh Hashanah and Yom Kippur. And I remember as kids we used to take out the *shofars* and try to blow them. Sometimes we were successful and could hear a screech.

At the back wall of the sanctuary was the Ark that contained the Torahs. There was an ornate wooden chair on each side of the Ark where my grandfather, as president of the shul, sat. I remember each September I would get a new dress to wear to synagogue and my new school shoes would be shined like new for synagogue. Shoes were bought at Noranda Shoe Store on 8th Street where they had the x-ray machine for checking the fit of the kids' shoes.

Balcony & Upper Room

A STAIRCASE LED UP to a large room and balcony. The room ran across the front of the building and was about eighteen feet deep. The balcony was the entire width of the building, and overlooked the Sanctuary. There was a curtain in front of part of the balcony where we would pin up bristol boards with the words (in phonetic English) to Hebrew songs we would sing. When there were religious services happening in the Sanctuary, some of the older, more traditional women would sit up on the balcony, even after the woman's section was established downstairs.

The room was furnished with utilitarian tables and chairs. It had two large cabinets that held all kinds of craft supplies (paper, pencils, pens, coloured pencils, bristol board, crayons, etc) and craft projects, finished and in process. It had two very old, worn out, moth-eaten couches with springs that didn't really work anymore, so when you sat on them, you sank way down. There may have been a record player and records as well. In this area, the kids gathered for Young Judaea to talk and do activities, usually on Sunday mornings. We also learned traditional Israeli folk dancing and singing, so it was great fun.

Basement

A STAIRCASE TO the left of the entrance hall led down to the basement. At the bottom of the stairs were two small washrooms and

a fully functional kitchen. The basement room itself was large and plain and was used somewhat like a community centre. At the back of the room was a stage with a piano where plays or other events happened. These events were usually led by Norma Miller who was active in arts and drama.

I can remember one year we put on a play for Purim about Haman's trial. Each child had a part. I was one of the guards who escorted Haman into the courtroom (not a speaking part, obviously). My cousin Kathy Korman also had a non-speaking part, playing Haman's girlfriend. She was made up like a tart and had to make sexy poses from time to time. Her brother, Harvey Korman, actually had a speaking part. His line was, "I like it, I like it," referring to peanut butter. It must have been very funny for the parents and adults watching.

On one side of the stage was the furnace room and on the other side was a small room with a few stairs up to the stage. The room was full of "stuff" and very dusty. At the back of this room was a door out

Purim play, circa 1949-1950. Back row, left to right: Pearl Fried, Meyer Isenberg, Julius Kitty, Henry Korman, Dolores Mednick. Seated: Tanya Garmaise, Lammy Sherman, Willie Korman, Shirley Rice, Rosalie Mednick, Marsha Sandberg. Front row (on floor), left to right: Florence Wiesenthal, Marilyn Ironstone.

Chanukah play, early 1950s. Front row: Isaac Korman (left), Hinda Mednick, Saul Korman, Sol Mednick, Willie Korman, Srul (Stanley) Pekelis. Seated in middle: Sylvia Scott, Sid Ritter, Faye Sandberg. Back row (standing): Ruth Ritter, Sally Scott, Vivian Ironstone, Murray Rice, Bunny Sherman. Photo by Ben Zifkin.

of the synagogue to the back lane.

A lot of community events happened in the basement. There were wedding and bar mitzvah parties when everyone came all dressed up and celebrated. The women usually prepared the food for these occasions in the kitchen. There were bazaar sales in the basement put on by the Hadassah women, with household items, clothing and hardware for sale. There were large Jewish community events when people from Val d'Or, Kirkland Lake, Timmins, North Bay, Sudbury and other towns would congregate.

As kids we were given free rein to have our own events at the shul. In high school, some good friends of mine formed a band, the Wildcats, and they used to practice in the basement. They performed at high school dances and at bars. My cousin, Jack Weinstein, was the manager and Harvey Korman played the sax.

This poor reproduction of Kneseth Israel's stationery from 1951 lists the members of its executive: Hon. President, Mike Korman; President, Louis Scott; Vice-President Nathan Wiesenthal; Secretary, Dr. H. R. Ironstone; Treasurer, Ben. Zifkin; Directors, M. J. Garmaise, Albert Isenberg, Sam Mednick.

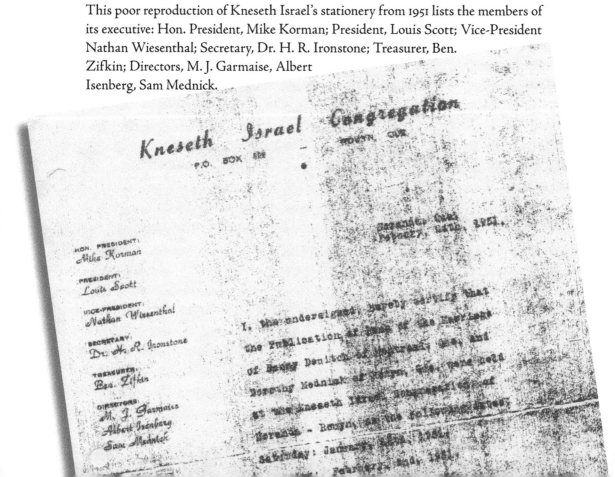

When I was in grade one, I started to take piano lessons with Mlle. Rouleau who lived on 8th Street. Until we got a piano in our house, I used to go to the synagogue to practice during school lunch hour. First, you have to know that I was (and still am) phobic about spiders, especially Daddy Long Legs. Unfortunately on the walls beside the staircase, and in the part of the basement with the bathrooms, there were millions of them (or so it seemed). In addition there were noises, creaks and clicks that were very loud (or so it seemed). I was *soooo* brave for a six-year-old, all alone in that building on the stage with the piano. I remember my mother telling me later in life that I used to tell her how scary it was, and that she didn't understand how I could do that by myself.

I remember during the Yom Kippur War of 1973, my husband, who was in the Israel Air Force at the time, told me he had heard on the Israeli radio that Rouyn–Noranda had sold their shul and donated the money to Israel for support during the war. Today the former shul is an apartment building. The outside still looks the same, with the Magen David in the window and the cornerstone still in place. §

Families

BLOWING THE SHOFAR ON ROSH HASHONOH

Left, Rabbi Osher Bloom, blowing the Shofar in the Noranda synagogue in 1954; and (above) in Rouyn–Noranda in 1949.

Our Teacher, Osher Bloom
by Ed Mednick

ON SATURDAY MORNINGS three or four of the children who were roughly seven to nine years of age like me would go to shul and stand on the *bimah* with Reverend Osher Bloom.

Osher (Oscar) Bloom was a teacher and spiritual leader who also conducted weddings. A Holocaust survivor, he spent five years in Rouyn–Noranda and then moved to the United States.

He would teach us how to *daven* and instruct us in the melodies for some of the Shabbos prayers and songs. It was, in retrospect, a great morning each week.

One Sunday dad asked me how shul had been the day before.

"Great," I replied.

"You weren't at shul yesterday," he said.

"How do you know?"

"I talked to Osher Bloom and he told me you weren't there as you usually are."

Rabbi Killed In Collision

(Special to The State Journal)

OWOSSO, June 28 — Rabbi Oscar Bloom, 26, of 300 Delia st., Flint, died this morning in Owosso Memorial hospital from injuries received Thursday night when he apparently fell asleep while driving on highway M-21, five miles west of Owosso.

Rabbi Bloom's car crossed the pavement and ran into two trees as his car was going east at Burton Corners.

Coroner Howard Jennings said that Rabbi Bloom died from internal injuries and a fractured skull.

DRIVER KILLED

OWOSSO, MICH., June 25 — (UP) — Oscar Bloom, 26, of Flint, was killed early today when his car ran off M-21 and struck two trees five miles west of here.

Reports from local Michigan newspapers tell of the tragic death of Rabbi Oscar (Osher) Bloom, former religious teacher in Rouyn–Noranda, who died in a car accident in 1957 at the age of twenty-six.

I confessed to my father that I had skipped shul and gone to the recreation centre to watch a hockey game. I loved hockey.

He replied, "Because you lied you cannot go to a hockey game at the arena for two months."

I never again missed shul on Saturday with Reverend Bloom. And I never lied to my father again!

Reverend Bloom treated me like his own child. He used to babysit me occasionally, as did Motel Smith.

Years later, he was tragically killed one night when he fell asleep at the wheel in Flint, Michigan, where he was to propose to his girlfriend. (This occurred after we had moved to Toronto.)

Interestingly, when we moved from Noranda he gave me a *Chumash* with his name inscribed in the inner cover with a note to me. When we sold our house in Toronto six years ago and moved to a condo, we had to give many of our books away. One of the few I kept was the *Chumash* from Reverend Bloom. §

Rouyn and Noranda Adventures
by Richard Clare

M Y MOM AND DAD, Cynthia and Lionel Clare, lived in Rouyn–Noranda from 1948 to 1960. Cynthia (nee Simon) was from Halifax, Nova Scotia. She moved to Montreal in her early twenties and worked in La Liberte department store on Notre Dame Street in St Henri. There she met my dad, Lionel Clare, who was in his late twenties and assistant manager of the store which was owned by his uncle Leo Feldman. Although he trained as a meteorologist, my father served in the Air Force during the war, then chose to work in retail with his uncle.

When my parents fell in love, Uncle Leo did not approve of two employees forming a couple. After my parents were married in 1948, my father found a job in Noranda working for Sam Bucovetsky's, a small department store with premises in both Noranda and Rouyn and with other outlets in Kirkland Lake and Timmins, Ontario. My mother also worked part time at the Noranda store. My father was hired by Myer Bucovetsky (who was later a professor of management at University of Toronto) to manage the two stores in Noranda and Rouyn, and eventually he became a superviser of operations for all the Ontario stores.

When my parents moved to Rouyn–Noranda they originally lived near Noranda Mines, not far from the Sam Bucovetsky store in Noranda. Then they moved to the New Townsite not far from MacNiven Elementary School. My parents had two children: Richard (aka Ricky — me) born in 1951, and Nancy born in 1955 (the last Jewish child born in Rouyn–Noranda). When we moved to Montreal in 1960, I was only nine years old but I have many fond memories from this period.

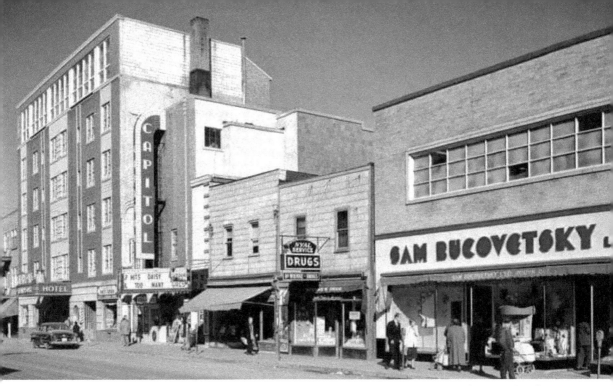

Lionel Clare managed the Sam Bucovetsky stores in Noranda and Rouyn (shown above).

The first thing I remember was that the Korman and Miller families played an important role in the community and were wonderful hosts. My father was a good friend of Isaac Korman and Harry Miller and my mother was a good friend of Rose Korman and Norma Miller. The Miller family had a cottage on Lake Dufault and we were often invited to the cottage to swim and toast marshmallows on an open fire. I remember that my parents liked to go fishing which they did at Rapid Seven (La Verendrye Wildlife Reserve) with their friends Jack and Becky Ritter.

The best memories I have was being invited to celebrate the High Holidays at Michel and Temel Korman's home. My favourite part of the celebration was that he encouraged the children to enjoy the red wine which was greatly appreciated by me as a seven- and eight-year-old. Even better, he would take us out from the house to throw pebbles into Lake Osisko in order to cast out our sins (the Jewish ritual known as *tachlis*). It also amused him to encourage us to shoot the pebbles at neighbours' windows which for an eight-year-old was a unique and wonderful opportunity!

Another thing that sticks in my mind was that my dad would occasionally walk with me on evenings near the Sam Bucovetsky store in Rouyn where there were nice (or not so nice) ladies of the night who were very friendly and who wore heavy make up. I could never understand why my dad who was normally very sociable would drag me quickly by the ear away from those lovely ladies of the night.

Another preferred activity of my father was to follow the volunteer firefighters to local fires. One day we followed the fire truck all around town by car to pick up the volunteers and then followed the fire truck to our own apartment. Turned out the fire was in our back yard where an abandoned car had caught on fire! Quite the surprise!

As a child I remember Esther and Jerry Korman as well as Marvin, Laurie and Debbie Miller, who were close to my age. However, we lost contact when we moved to Montreal. I was very sad to move to Montreal at nine years old and cried all the way. I hated that city because I missed all of my friends, all the houses were stuck together, and there was no nearby lake where we would be invited!

Finally I remember the Fried and Katz families and vaguely remember buying kosher meat with my parents at the Fried's butcher store. My Rouyn–Noranda experience was very formative and I have very fond memories living in that community where people were very close-knit, friendly and caring. Montreal was more impersonal, and though it offered strong educational opportunities it did not have the warmth of the Rouyn–Noranda community. §

Fried Family History
by Ruth (Fried) Drazin

MY FATHER, Moishe (Sam) Fried arrived in Rouyn–Noranda in 1936 from Romania, thanks to the sponsorship of our uncle, Rabbi Mendel Katz. (My mother, Gitel, and Rabbi Katz's wife, Golda, were sisters.) Permission was granted because he was going to be the kosher butcher for the Jewish community of Rouyn–Noranda. The family — our mother and children Pearl, Isaac and Mair — came in the fall of 1938 on board one of the last ships leaving Europe before WW2.

They left Romania by train accompanied by Mendel Pollak to insure their safety. Mendel was the husband of my mother's sister Chaya Sara and the father of Mair Pollak (see page 208). He could only travel with them as far as Trieste, where he assisted in the travel arrangements for the train to the port of Brest in Western France. There, they boarded the ship that would take them to Quebec City.

Once there, they took the train to Senneterre and then on to Rouyn. Two more children were born to our parents in Rouyn — Max in 1939 and I (Ruth) in 1941.

After they reached bar mitzvah age, the boys went to the Lubavitch Yeshiva in Montreal. Isaac became a well respected doctor, an ear, nose and throat specialist at the Jewish General Hospital in Montreal. Mair went into business, and Max continued our family tradition as a livestock dealer. Pearl and Ruth married and resided in Montreal to be close to the whole family.

The Fried family appreciated the friendliness of the total community towards them as well as their offspring. The respect for each other was mutual. We are grateful to *Hashem* for all our blessings and we *"schepp nachas"* from all our children, grandchildren and great grandchildren who are living in Israel, New York, New Jersey and Montreal. §

A Northern Sojourn
by Malcolm Finkelman

Winter, 8th Street, Rouyn–Noranda. Sam Mednick Grocery, Meat and Beer at left.

THE STORY OF THE FINKELMAN clan in Northern Ontario and Northwestern Quebec during the twentieth century is a classic immigrants' history. Its roots trace a path back to the Baltic region, Poland and northern Romania in the nineteenth century.

The maternal side of the family, the Katz family, lived in Sighet, a city on the border of Ukraine. Sighet had a Jewish community that thrived during the pre-World War Two period but it perished in the Holocaust. My grandfather, Rabbi Mendel Katz, left for England in the late 1920s and by 1932, had moved on to Canada and was able to send for his wife Golda and children, two daughters, Youlanne (Yentl, my mother), her twin Edith, and a son, Mair. Three more sons, Reuben, Max and Isaac, followed in Canada. An ordained rabbi, Mendel Katz took up a pulpit in the northern Quebec mining town of Rouyn–Noranda where he and Golda raised their family.

The paternal side of the family, the Finkelmans, had emigrated from Disna, Belarus to Riga, Latvia at the beginning of the twentieth century. Sam (Simcha) Finkelman left the troubled post–World War One Latvia and arrived in Timmins, Ontario in 1920, where he had an older brother and relatives from another branch of the family. While there, he met and married Hannah Greenberg whose family had emigrated from the environs of Warsaw to Montreal and then to Timmins. They began their lives as business people and soon my father, Victor (Avigdor) Finkelman, came along.

In 1926, they moved to nearby Kirkland Lake, then a newly developing mining town. There, the Finkelman family grew to six children including Victor, Sydney, Mary, Reta, Murray and Sharon. The towns where my parents grew up, Kirkland Lake and Rouyn–Noranda, were located about eighty-five kilometers apart and the Ontario–Quebec border was about midway between them. They were also seriously out in the wilderness, as James Bay was about 320 kilometers to the north. Toronto was about 630 kilometers to the south and Montreal was about 630 kilometers to the southeast.

Thriving in the North

THE TWO FAMILIES settled in their respective communities during their respective pioneer days. Copper mining was the primary industry in both towns and with all of the secondary industry, commercial and support services, both were booming in the twenties through the fifties. Hard-working and hardy people were needed for every facet of life. Both towns had small but vibrant Jewish communities comprised of business people and professionals and each supported an Orthodox synagogue as soon as they could afford it.

Our nuclear family was a hybrid with strong links to both Rouyn (my mother) and Kirkland Lake (my father). My parents, Youlanne Katz and Victor Finkelman, married in 1948 (see their wedding photo on page 61); my sister Faith came along in 1950 and I was born in 1952, both of us in Kirkland Lake. My father had come home from service in

Notices of the Jewish High Holidays often
appeared in the local press, as in these news items from 1946 and 1947.
"Visitors from Malartic, Val d'Or, Duparquet, Cobalt and other places again came
to the little frame synagogue on Eighth St., Noranda for the services," the Rouyn–
Noranda Press reported in 1947.

the Royal Canadian Air Force in World War Two and had gone into
business with his father, Sam, who, in addition to his businesses in
Kirkland Lake, had a small hotel in Virginiatown, Ontario. "V-town"
was situated almost on the Ontario–Quebec border halfway between
Rouyn and Kirkland Lake. We moved to Virginiatown for a couple
of years and then to Rouyn. Our lives were defined by trips back and
forth between the three communities along an eighty-five kilometre
stretch of highway through the bush.

Life in these small towns, as viewed through the lens of
memory, was idyllic for kids. We came and went as we pleased with
little supervision. Our playgrounds were the forests, lakes, trails, and
most enticingly, seriously dangerous abandoned mine workings. Six-
year-olds being sent off to school on a forty-below February morning
was no big deal. I have said many times that our childhoods back then
were governed by the character-building principles of benign neglect

and reckless endangerment. This did not extend to our educational activities however. For us Jewish kids, being from immigrant or first generation households, studying was of ultimate importance and it was expected that we would become accomplished from the word go. It did not hurt that by the time many of us got to grade one (who ever heard of kindergarten) we could speak English, French, and Yiddish. Basic reading proficiency in English at that age was not uncommon and we were also attending cheder to do it all in Hebrew, but from right to left!

Both my sister and I attended the Rouyn Protestant School which was two blocks from our house. I remember the look on the first grade teacher's face when three of us asked if she had any more books by the time she finished handing out the readers. The cheder was a mile away in Noranda, in the shul, where Mr. Sharony would try his best with the no-goodniks he had been dealt. Walking to cheder in the winter was an experience whose memory still causes me to wince. After my bar mitzvah in Noranda on May 15, 1965, I was also expected to show up and help make a minyan, which were often difficult to assemble, for various observances and yahrtzeits.

The pulse of the Jewish communities was maintained by their shuls. The shuls were their beating hearts. Here the community *davened*, observed the High Holy Days, passed Jewish learning to the youngsters, celebrated bar mitzvahs and occasional weddings, and met in their various communal organizations. I remember fondly singing Hatikvah at Young Judaea meetings at the shul in Noranda. I will admit to yearning, during the winter with the heat set low, that this Jewish spirit could be someplace warmer. Yiddishkeit was maintained in daily life and the cycle of *Yomim Tovim* (Jewish holidays). In Rouyn–Noranda, like Kirkland Lake, kosher meat arrived by overnight train from Toronto or Montreal. Elite chocolate bars at Passover were a very special treat. The needs of a Jewish community were met.

The sixties were the period of the "great dwindle." Both

communities suffered the effects of kids going off to school in Toronto and Montreal and settling in the south. In addition, parents eventually moved closer to their kids, accelerating the decline. Finally, economic conditions deteriorated with mine closures and the loss of the English population in general. This spelled the beginning of the end for the Jewish communities of Kirkland Lake and Rouyn–Noranda. Businesses and practices closed and the former pioneers headed south. Ultimately, both shuls closed and were eventually converted to multi-unit dwellings. Plaques remain to declare that Jews once *davened* here. After returning briefly to Kirkland Lake where both my sister and I finished high school, we moved to Toronto. Our Kirkland Lake grandparents resettled in retirement in Toronto and our grandmother from Rouyn, in Montreal. Our parents settled in North York and to their chagrin, my sister went off to McGill and I attended Western.

The Northern Diaspora

THE JEWISH COMMUNITIES of Rouyn–Noranda and Kirkland Lake were born of the great European cataclysms of the twentieth century. The immigrants who peopled those communities were engaged in a literal existential quest. Their survival and flourishing, against long odds and difficult circumstances, is testimony to their grit and steadfastness. Those of us who were raised by them in those northern towns have many fond memories of the vanished Jewish communities. Times were certainly simpler and the future was full of promise. As we occasionally gather, our meetings, recollections and anecdotes may be sweeter than merited, but they are the memories of our youth and we will continue to cherish them. §

Left to right: Max Martin, Mr. and Mrs. Tom Mallin, and Sonia and Max Garmaise in Kirkland Lake, circa 1948. [OJA]

Reminiscences of the Jewish Community
by Mona (Garmaise) Klein

I WANT TO CONTRIBUTE TO the collection of memories and history we have together. It is wonderful to be reconnected to voices and remembrances. Somehow we remember each other clearly even after the passage of many years.

I am writing about my parents, Max and Sonia Garmaise, and their three children, Tanya (Feldman), Mona (Klein), and David.

Max, born in Montreal, became a lawyer, and practised in Montreal together with A.M. Klein. They had a lot of fun, but couldn't make a living. It was Depression time in the 1930s. Klein was travelling all over Canada trying to raise money for the creation of the State of Israel. He spoke in Noranda, and signalled to Max that the community needed a lawyer. Max was the unmarried one at the time. He agreed to the move. He came to Rouyn–Noranda in 1935 with $50 in his pocket, opened an office with Klein and lived in the office. It wasn't long before Klein and Garmaise were doing better than they

A. M. Klein practiced law in partnership with Max Garmaise in Rouyn–Noranda in 1936. After that he returned to Montreal and made his name as a celebrated poet and novelist.

had in Montreal. Max married Sonia in 1936. The Kleins and the Garmaises lived together on First Avenue for a year. They had a ball. After that A.M. returned to Montreal.

Tanya was born in 1937, Mona in 1944, David in 1947. We lived at 69 Tremoy Road and 14 – 6th Street. My parents often recounted how much they enjoyed life in Noranda. They were young and energetic, and the community was close. Esther Sandberg taught others how to bake — and oh, what strudel and cookies! And Max began his community work right from the beginning. He gave talks on Remembrance Day, got involved in local politics, aided displaced persons and immigrants, and even offered counseling to couples before handling a divorce.

Couples came to him because he was Jewish, and therefore not Roman Catholic where divorce was impossible religiously. His last enduring work was the establishment of a Centre d'Acceuil. He was by then a judge in the social welfare court. Not bad for an Anglo Jew in a French Catholic town!

I remember a number of occasions where my father educated judges about Jewish rituals. He protected and lobbied for the rights of our religious community members. I remember being very proud of him. And the judges were willing to learn. I know he changed the practice of the community when it came to remuneration for our Rabbi Katz so that he received a regular salary each week. It was important to recognize and honour the dignity of each individual, and he repeated that with immigrants and others who needed landed immigrant status.

My mother, Sonia, was my father's office manager. Her shorthand was amazing. And she also opened a store called Foureurs Bernard, which sold furs and upscale women's clothing in a salon style, with sofas and display tables par excellence. That business didn't lose money, but it didn't profit either.

I remember life on Tremoy Road. We played outside in the back lane every night. We jumped from garage roofs into snow banks. We put on little plays. Admission was one diaper pin. Every week day I would go to cheder. I wrote my name in Hebrew before I could write it in English. I remember several teachers (we defeated most of them). But Mr. Sharony stands out. When my father would come to inspect, we would be angels. Then he would leave. Chaos!

Sunday mornings were for Young Judaea, immersing us in songs, Israeli dances, artwork, lessons, and many other creative activities. We also heard "*sichot*," which were talks about Israel and significant figures such as Ben Gurion, Jabotinsky, and Herzl. We had impressive congresses. Once we put together a dance troupe and performed at the Recreation Center. A man, scouting in Noranda, found me walking home, and expressed his amazement that we had such a developed and tight group.

Young Judaea was run by our older kids as a form of leadership practice. Upon reflection, we took it for granted, but really it is quite impressive, how loyal we were, how we took on responsibility and organized ourselves. We taught each other in Young Judaea. We committed to our Sunday mornings, week after week, and by sixteen years of age, we were leaders. We have so many memories of the multitude of creative activities we organized together. We kept our Jewish community close with energy and commitment.

I remember that I had to have my eyes checked at a very young age. In order to do that, we had to fly to Montreal to see Dr. Eisenman. That meant we boarded an army plane on Lake Osisko. Two benches lined up opposite each other, with large cups stowed under our legs in case of nausea. That was inevitable. We stopped in Val d'Or, in Ottawa and then in Montreal. I remember my mother changing my clothes on the plane, and that I felt very shy about it.

We would walk across Lake Osisko in the winter, from Noranda to Rouyn, because it was shorter. It was often very very cold, although people didn't seem to complain about it too much. I would get to Martin's Menswear on Main Street to thaw out. It was warm and inviting, and people seemed to congregate there. And someone would say to me, "Mona, your nose is frozen," which wasn't a surprise, and I would rub it and tolerate the itching.

I remember parties in the shul. I remember Michel Korman, a rotund man, dancing! He loved it, and would move his feet with joy. He was a man who didn't really say much, but could let go and we watched with amazement. I remember putting on plays at the shul. Young Judaea would do its thing and bring a lot of laughter from the audience, which was the whole community. And adults would put on skits. There would be refreshments galore pouring out of the kitchen.

And that brings to mind my mother's stories about learning how to bake; Esther Sandberg was the expert. They all succeeded in baking everything from bagels to strudel to danish to cakes. My mother would send me to Noranda Bakery to ask Mrs. Jahnevitch for ten cents worth of yeast. The cinnamon and sugar, and jam and nuts that went into that strudel!

Of course, we walked everywhere. Almost no one had a car. Max Martin may have been the first. A taxi ride anywhere cost fifty cents.

There was no such thing as a carpool. We came home from school for lunch, and went back for the afternoon. Very very few snowdays. We were used to the wall of snow in the morning at the front door, the bottles of milk proud with their iced raised caps.

On the way from Noranda to Rouyn we could stop at a chip stand and buy fries. We would douse them with vinegar and salt, and eat them as we walked. The vinegar would seep through the paper bag and we would enjoy it all, even the wet paper at the end. Ten cents a bag.

For Passover, a huge community order would arrive by freight overnight from Toronto. It would be divided as per each family's order. I remember eggs arriving in a big crate, and I would transfer them to cartons, and families would come and collect them. We would haul out our Passover dishes, a motley crew of single pieces, which each year we would recognize and delight.

Some of us would go to Camp Shalom or Camp Hagshama in the summers. It was our parents' wish to immerse us in a Jewish environment. We'd go by train, stop in North Bay to transfer in the midde of the night. No qualms.

It is so wonderful that we retained our Jewish identity, almost as if nothing could shake it.

Often we were the only Jews in our class. In grade eight Norman Wiesenthal was with me in science class. The teacher once berated us: "You two! You are always asking questions which are not in the book!" As if only the Jews did that.

We were not a materialistic community. We had books, games, and cards and not much decor. Nobody was rich, although certainly some were poorer than others. Coming to the big city was a shock.

The problem with Noranda was that we were remote. We knew it. It was a ten-to-twelve hour bus ride to Montreal, and the road was gravel for a long time. Living in Noranda meant that once you finished high school, you left. No university, no post-secondary education then. And our parents knew it.

Aerial view of the original synagogue, center (building with two-tone roof), with smokestacks of Noranda Mines dominating the horizon.

The small town had become a place where there was not enough cultural stimulation, no concerts, no theatre. And so in adolescence we always had the sense of our future lying outside of Noranda. How difficult that was for our parents. They were empty-nested very early. I was sixteen when I graduated. I would come back for holidays, and after university terms ended, and one summer I worked as a secretary at Noranda Mines for which I was totally unqualified (but I brought life to the accounting department). Some parents began to follow their children. They saw opportunity in the big city now. And the community began to dwindle. I know that was sad for my parents when their good friends moved away.

I was so touched when Isaac Katz told me he returned to teach at Noranda High School for a couple of years, and how much he enjoyed it. §

View of A. D. Carmichael Elementary School (originally known as Noranda Elementary School).

Fond Memories of Rouyn–Noranda
by Sol Goldstein

IT WAS IN THE FALL OF 1943 when my mother embarked, along with my brothers Aaron aged seven, Kalman aged three, and me aged five, upon the train trip from Melville, Saskatchewan: a two-night and three-day trip aboard a train packed with soldiers and their repeated refrains of "*You Are My Sunshine.*" My father had already established himself in Rouyn–Noranda where he was the Hebrew teacher and Rabbi.

Our first apartment was on Third Avenue above the bowling alley. In the neighbouring unit, was the Ginsberg family — the Jewish butcher. My early memories there are of huge snowstorms with the snow being packed down by enormous rollers drawn by horses. Ploughs were restricted only to the main streets. It was here that I first saw this fabulous machine called a snowmobile. Cheder was in a rented space on Third Avenue. The bakery was on Second Avenue and 9th Street. The new shul was being constructed on 9th Street.

The milkman was Mr. Kravitz who delivered milk from his horse-drawn sled; it was pasteurized milk since homogenized had not yet been invented. He also had great cottage cheese and cream. He would leave the milk at the front door early in the morning and by the time my mother would retrieve it, the milk had frozen and risen about six inches above the bottle openings. It was a real sight to behold five quarts of milk, lined up with their protruding tops, and the bottle cork perched gingerly at the very top. His horse's name was Dyanyah. The greatest excitement occurred when the horse was spooked and would run away, scattering contents of the sled or wagon along the street.

The police chief was Mr. Charlebois. I recall it being newsworthy that he was only twenty-six years old when appointed. The vice-chief-constable was Mr. Foubault. On occasion, there would be a wrestling match between the two of them as part of a sports show in Noranda.

When the shul was being built, the president being Michel Korman, one could find the occasional pile of cow dung in the backyard, left there by a cow who had escaped the Fried herd. Important phone numbers which I remember were the Mednick family (113), the Rice family (133), Dr. Pauly (5), Noranda Taxi (333) and the Martin family (143).

Upon termination of my father's contract, my family decided to stay and open a business, Marsha's Dry Goods at 139 – 8th Street. This new store was furnished with counters given to us by Joe Mednick, which came from his store which had been closed down as a result of a fire a few years earlier.

We moved to the apartment behind the store, a convenient location as it was half way between Joe Korman's grocery store on one side and Mednick's grocery store on the other. This was a particularly exciting location as it was across the street from the home of Bill Mucha, the goaltender for the Noranda Tigers, later called the Noranda Copper Kings. His girlfriend, Miss Thorslund, was my

View of Noranda High School.

grade four teacher.

My school teachers in Noranda Elementary School were Miss Myhill in grade one; Miss Bunt in grade two; Miss Larrett in grade three; Miss Thorslund in grade four; Miss Fleming in grade five; Miss Judd in grade six (her name was changed to Mrs. Bell when she married in the middle of the school year); and Miss Brown in grade seven.

In Noranda High School, our grade eight teacher was Miss Lillian Baker, a great teacher with a sternness that kept everyone in the classroom in line, even the transient visitors who were there only during the cold of winter when they could not work as loggers. She was the only one who could control the biggest guy in the class, Kent Douglas, who later played for the Toronto Maple Leafs and won a Calder Memorial Trophy.

Sam Mednick, the owner of Mednick's Grocery Store, gave me my

Sam Mednick of Mednick's Grocery Store.

first stick of gum. It was spearmint, a taste I will never forget. When I visited his store when he was there, I was encouraged to reach into the box containing the chocolate and marshmallow cookies: "Here Sol, take another one."

Mr. Zifkin, the photographer, had a studio and a dark room which was four doors from Marsha's Dry Goods. My brothers and I would go there to cool off after we had been engaged in a heated game of hockey outside in the freezing cold. He would feed me pumpernickel bread and salami, a secret between us as my mother considered this unhealthy food and therefore contraband. He would tell us wonderful stories and gave me lessons on how to develop pictures from a negative. He exuded a great deal of warmth and I recall him as the grandfather I never had. In the summer, he would be visited by his grandchildren from Toronto and I recall being told by them about wonderful Toronto, a city which had several parks and not just one like Noranda. They also had traffic lights — a real wonder because you had to stop when the light was red and go when the light was green. I remember questioning what would happen if the green light turned red and you were caught in the middle. These visits with Mr. Zifkin also posed a problem in that, within fifteen minutes of eating the salami and upon my coming home, my mother would greet us with cookies and milk. What was I to do about the law of not mixing milk and meat, all within ten minutes of one another? Oh well, I survived in spite of this sin.

As a young boy, I always perceived Zelda Mednick to be strict as an adult and assigned her much power. One summer day, there was a storm in Noranda. The winds were powerful enough that they blew the signs off the roof of Belisle's Hardware, a frightening occurrence. The next day, I heard that Mrs. Mednick had given birth to her baby. I put the two of them together as this was her power and that is how the baby came. That baby was Ed Mednick, who became a well-known and successful ophthalmologist in Toronto.

My brother Aaron's bar mitzvah was in March 1949. The entire community participated. Each family came with a special dish they had prepared for the celebration. Lazar Kitty, who owned the beverage company, supplied all the pop for the occasion. I remember Sonya Korman, the mother of Saul Korman, teaching my mother how to bake a chocolate cake, something for which I thanked her for years to come, well into my adulthood.

My best friend was Willie Korman, one of Simcha and Dvoshe's four sons. Willie was also the uncle of Gordon Korman, the famous author of children's books which were all very popular in the 1970s and 1980s. Gordon Korman is still very popular and has just published his hundredth book. It was also a privilege to be Willie's friend for two other reasons. His mother always had treats for us when I came to their house. I even had the choice of either an orange or a chocolate popsicle, or sometimes got both. Willie was also the ace pitcher of the JP baseball team, the top team in Noranda.

Two months after my bar mitzvah in Noranda on May 5, 1951, our family moved away. Since 1968 I've been living in Toronto, where I was a staff psychiatrist with the department of child psychiatry at Sick Children's Hospital. As I write this I am almost eighty-four years old, and regard myself as forever a Noranda alumnus. §

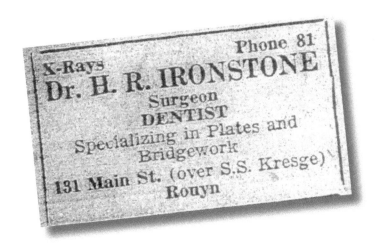

Some Ironstone History
by Vivian (Ironstone) Field

OUR FATHER, DR. HARRY IRONSTONE, graduated from McGill University in dentistry about 1932. He decided to set up a practice in Rouyn–Noranda. To that end, he went there to see the possibilities. I understand that he initially went in by canoe! He met my mother, Toby Friedman of Ansonville, at a Jewish wedding in Timmins. They were married in Kirkland Lake.

Three children followed: Vivian (me), Marilyn (now deceased) and Norman. We lived at 22 – 9th street (across from Eddie and Rae Rice). My father's first practice was in that house. Our house was next door to the synagogue. When Norman arrived, we had outgrown that house and so we moved to 73 Tremoy Road.

My father set up his practice in the Kay Joseph Building in Rouyn and was there for many years. He realized that smaller communities like Malartic and Val d'Or did not have dental services so he went to those communities one day a week for many years. (The drill he used was operated by foot pedal!) Those communities were primarily Francophone, however, and he did not speak the language. Eventually, he had a stroke and was forced to retire.

The children grew up and after high school went off to seek higher education. Norman's bar mitzvah was a huge celebration! Vivian went to McGill and then graduated as a registered nurse at Toronto's Womens College Hospital. Marilyn went to McDonald College to become a teacher, Norman to McGill School of Dentistry.

Our family's years in Noranda were full. Our parents curled, golfed, had great parties and were involved in all aspects of community life, both Jewish and otherwise. My father was district governor for the Lions Club and represented the area at a convention in New York City. We all participated in many school activities, debate teams, Young Judaea. Vivian was class valedictorian at graduation.

An update: Vivian lives independently in Sudbury. Marilyn was widowed young in Sudbury, moved to Toronto, had a double lung transplant and, sadly, passed away about ten years ago. Norman is retired and living in Ottawa. §

Albert & Sarah (Mednick) Isenberg in the year of their marriage (1932).

The Isenberg–Mednick Family
by Meyer and Miriam Isenberg

T HE HISTORY OF the Isenberg and Mednick family and how they ended up in Rouyn–Noranda is interesting.

Albert Isenberg was born in Russia in 1909 on Simchas Torah. His father Hershel had left Russia before World War One to start a new life in Canada. He eventually settled in Winnipeg. It had always been his intention to bring his family over, but Albert's mother, Miriam (Lumden) Isenberg, died of the Spanish flu, leaving Albert an orphan. His father saved enough money to send for his son, but the trip to Canada was very difficult. He was denied entry to the ship as a result of an eye infection and ended up living on the streets of Belgium for ten months before coming to Canada. His father had saved enough for a second ticket. Albert worked in Winnipeg, Guelph and Cochrane before meeting his beloved wife, Sarah Mednick.

Sarah was born in 1911 in David Gorodek, Pinsk Gubernia, Russia (now in Belarus). Her mother, Esther Mirrel Mednick, was part of a large well-known family, the Kormans. Sarah's two older brothers,

Albert Isenberg with his father Hershel Isenberg (wearing the fedora) and his son outside Albert's Mens Wear, date unknown.

Joe and Sam Mednick, had left Russia in 1921 and settled initially in Englehart, then in Timmins, and finally in Noranda. They sponsored their sisters Sarah and Dorothy, brother Beryl and their mother. They all settled in Timmins which is where she met Albert Isenberg.

Albert and Sarah were married in 1932 and shortly thereafter moved to Rouyn–Noranda. They rented a house in Noranda and Sarah's mother and sister lived with them. Esther Mirrel died in 1940.

After their first son Saul was born in 1933, they moved to a house on Taschereau Street in Rouyn. Two more sons were born, Meyer in 1937 and Irving in 1943. In order to support his growing and extended family Albert opened a menswear store on Perreault Street East. He later built a menswear store, The Varsity, on Main Street next to Nathan Wiesenthal's grocery store. He also built a sixplex in the New Townsite and later opened a store in La Sarre, Quebec. His last store was in Cochrane, Ontario — Albert's Mens Wear — which he later sold to Ben Miller from Rouyn.

Sam & Esther Mirrel with son Beryl
in Noranda, circa late 1920s.

In the early 1970s, Albert and Sarah relocated to Toronto to be closer to their family and friends. They took great pleasure in their grandchildren. Albert passed away in 1998 and Sarah in 2005.

LIFE FOR THE ISENBERG family was always busy and interesting. Albert was busy with his store(s) and often went on buying trips. He was also involved with the synagogue which he helped build and was its president one year. Sarah looked after her mother and their three sons. She was also involved with the synagogue and Hadassah; since she was fluent in English, Hebrew, Yiddish and French, she would often introduce out-of-town speakers. She was also an avid reader: they nicknamed her the *culturno* — "the cultured one."

Although Dorothy initially lived with the Isenbergs she later moved to Quebec City where her brother Beryl was a rabbi. She met and married Danny Deuitch in Noranda. They had one child, Mirrel.

Life in Rouyn–Noranda with its small but active Jewish community was good. Sarah had many relatives in the Mednick-Korman community. However, the Isenbergs were concerned about the future of their sons. They sent Saul to yeshiva in New York to further his Jewish learning. Meyer and Irving initially went to Rouyn

Deuitch–Mednick Wedding, February 24, 1952, Rouyn–Noranda.
❧ Front Row, from left (sitting on floor): Eddie Mednick, Stanley Mednick.
❧ Middle row: Irving Isenberg, Meyer Isenberg, Rosalie Mednick, Hinda Mednick, Sol Mednick.
❧ Back row: Sam & Zelda Mednick, Saul Isenberg, Rabbi Beryl Mednick, Danny Deuitch (groom), Dorothy Mednick Deuitch (bride), Sarah & Albert Isenberg, Rae & Joe Mednick.

Protestant School and high school in Noranda, but all three sons later moved to Toronto. All went to post graduate studies with Saul becoming a pharmacist, Meyer a psychiatrist, and Irving a chartered accountant.

In 1957, Saul married Beverley and they had three children: Ellen who followed in her father's footsteps as a pharmacist, and Laurie and Stephen. The two daughters live in Israel and have very extensive families. Sadly, both Saul and Beverley died young, Saul in 2000 and Beverley in 2013.

The Isenberg Family in Toronto, 1988. Seated, from left: Saul, Beverley, Sarah, Albert. Standing, from left: Irving, Denise, Mayer, Miriam.

In 1969 Meyer married Miriam; they have two children, Hartley and Jacqueline (Jody), and four grandchildren.

In 1970 Irving married Denise and they had two children, Jillian and James, and one grandson.

Although life could be hard there are some memories that last forever.

Meyer's bar mitzvah in 1950 was scheduled to coincide with Dolores Mednick and Morrie Bloch's wedding so out-of-town families would not have to travel twice. His most popular line was "Today I am a fountain pen" as that was the favourite gift.

On Simcha Torah the families would go to the synagogue and then visit other families' homes to celebrate.

Stephen, the son of Saul and Beverley Isenberg, remembers hearing about his father and his friends playing hockey on the ice. Dave Keon, who was much younger, always wanted to join in, but they refused. Even at a young age Keon, who went on to become a hockey icon, was better and more skilled than the much older players. §

Wedding of Edith Katz and Rabbi David Spiro, Montreal, October 1945. Behind the bride and groom are: Youlanne Katz (left), Golda & Rabbi Menachem Katz, Ruben Katz. Seated in front: Max Katz (left), Isaac Katz.

Rabbi Katz & the Katz Family
by Dr. Isaac Katz

M Y FATHER, RABBI Alter Menachem Zev Katz, who served as Rouyn–Noranda's resident Jewish spiritual leader for nearly two decades, was born in Hungary in 1899. At that time Hungary was part of the Austro-Hungarian Empire, which possessed a large Jewish community and attracted many Jews from other parts of Europe. But when the eastern two-thirds of Hungary was given to Romania after the First World War, conditions became harsh for the Jewish population.

My father and my mother Golda were married when they were quite young. Twin girls, Edith and Youlanne, were followed by a son,

Mair. My father was studying at yeshiva to be a rabbi. They were supported by my mother's father who was a wealthy man.

My father, seeing no future for himself and his family, decided to leave Romania. He travelled to London, England, where he taught cheder for one year, became a landed immigrant, and learned English. He then came to Canada and completed his studies in Winnipeg and went to Toronto to learn *schita* (ritual slaughter). After this, he came to Montreal where he met up with his friend, Joseph Schreter, also from Romania.

By the late 1920s, a small Jewish community consisting of merchants, businessmen and professionals had arisen in Rouyn–Noranda. The Canadian Jewish Congress, which attempted to allocate resources where they were most needed, asked my father to go to Rouyn–Noranda to be the Rabbi for the community. He arrived in 1930.

When my father moved to Rouyn–Noranda, he was waiting to be reunited with his family who were still in Romania. On June 27, 1932, my mother and the children arrived in Quebec City aboard the *Empress of Australia*. She took the train to Senneterre and horse and buggy to Rouyn–Noranda, where the family was reunited. Three more children were born in Rouyn: Ruben, Max and I (Isaac).

As the Rabbi, my father was earning a meagre salary and my mother saw that they could not make it with this level of income. Back in Sighet, Hungary, she had learned to manage her father's store so he could conduct other business during the day. She was also a seamstress. In Rouyn, she decided to open a clothing store. She traveled to Montreal to buy the goods wholesale from Mr. Schreter to sell retail in Rouyn. This was how we were able to grow up and be provided for.

As the *chazzan*, my father conducted the services on the High Holidays and throughout the year. He also taught the bar mitzvah boys and after-school cheder classes. He conducted the wedding

Wedding of Victor Finkelman & Youlanne Katz, August 1948. Left to right: Ruben Katz, Mair Katz, Golda Katz, groom & bride, Rabbi Menachem Katz, Edith Spiro, Rabbi David Spiro. In front: Isaac Katz (seated), Max Katz (standing).

ceremonies but could not officiate at funerals because he was a Kohen. He also served as the *schoichet*, ritually slaughtering cows and chickens so that the community could have kosher meat. When this was no longer feasible, the community ordered its kosher meat from Toronto and sometimes Montreal.

Eventually, the community hired other spiritual leaders to conduct services, teach cheder and instruct the bar mitzvah boys. My father died in July 1950. Afterwards, the community would hire a *chazzan* from Montreal or Toronto for the High Holidays. He would invariably stay at the hotel owned by Mr. Joseph Korman and have his meals with our family and the Fried family.

In the 1940s, as many as forty-five Jewish families were part of our congregation and our community. As the children left to continue their education in Montreal and Toronto, their parents also began to relocate to be close to their families. The synagogue was closed in 1972 and the building sold to the Lions Club.

WITHIN OUR FAMILY, my sister Edith, of blessed memory, was the first to marry. It was a real *shidach*. She met her future groom in Montreal in April 1945 and was engaged the same week. The wedding took place six months later, in October. Her husband was Rabbi David Spiro, the rabbi of Fredericton, New Brunswick. Their three children were Micheal, Marilyn and Helene.

My sister Youlanne, of blessed memory, married Victor Finkelman, a young man from Kirkland Lake, in August 1948. They moved to the small mining town of Virginiatown, just over the border in Ontario, where he managed a small hotel. The family moved to Rouyn where the children, Faith and Malcolm, attended school. They then moved to Toronto where Victor worked in the insurance business.

My older brother Mair, of blessed memory, was born in Europe. When he was seventeen and in Canada, he decided, together with two high school friends, to enlist in the Army, the Black Watch (Royal Highland Regiment). It was 1944, the war was still raging, and it was not uncommon for boys of that age to enlist. My father tried to get him out but to no avail. Luckily, Mair was on the docks in Halifax waiting to board a troop ship when the war ended. The Army trained him as an electrician before he was discharged. He came home and worked in the mines. Sadly, he passed away in 2003 and is greatly missed. He never married and lived with my mother and helped her in her old age.

My brother Ruben was studying at yeshiva in Montreal when our father died. He came home and decided not to return to yeshiva and finished high school in Noranda. After graduation he went to work for the railroad. He then moved to Montreal and was employed in various office jobs. He and his wife Shirley had three children,

Above, Rabbi Katz and Ruben Katz, 1948. At right, Isaac Katz, attending Noranda High School at age 16, with his dog Kelef. Isaac found him sleeping in a snowbank and rescued him.

Sherry, Marla and Darren. He died tragically in 1975 and this was a great shock to the family. He was only forty-two years old.

My brother Max graduated McGill Medical School in 1964. He became a hematologist and accomplished a fifty-one-year career in medicine. He was affiliated with the Royal Victoria Hospital and Lakeshore General Hospital in Montreal. During his career he was an associate professor of Medicine in the McGill Faculty of Medicine. His family consists of his wife Kirsten Miriam and daughters Signe and Nili.

I graduated from the McGill Faculty of Dentistry in 1970. I went to the Boston University of School of Graduate Dentistry and became an endodontist. I accomplished a fifty-year career in dentistry. I was also a faculty lecturer in the McGill Faculty of Dentistry. My family consists of my wife Nancy and children Melissa, Jason and Robyn. We are also blessed with six grandchildren. §

❧ *Photo: The Shlaime & Soreh Korman Family*
Rouyn–Noranda, circa 1931

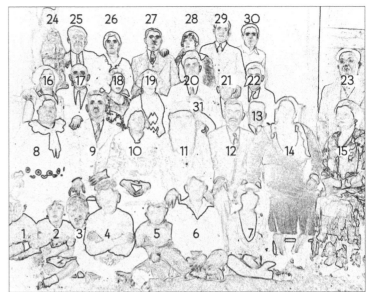

This magnificent Korman family portrait was taken in Rouyn–Noranda about 1931. Patriarch and matriarch Shlaime and Soreh Korman are in the middle (positions 11 & 12), surrounded by most of their children (names in bold) and some of their grandchildren.

❧ Front row, left to right: (1) Henry, (2) Fanny (Weinstein) and (4) Isaac, children of Temel & Michel; (3) unknown; (5) Willie, son of Sonya & Nachman; (6) Jack and (7) Lilly (Cartman), children of Esther & A.J.

❧ Second row (from bottom), left to right: (8) Sheindel, (9) **Joe**, (10) Soreh ("The Bobbe") & (11) Shlaime, (12) **David**, (13) Sidney Sandberg (nephew of Shlaime and Soreh), (14) Chane-Fagel, (15) Dasha.

❧ Third row (from bottom), left to right: (16) Sonya & (17) **Itzik**, (18) Rae (Rice, Sonia & Itzik's), (19) Sonya & (20) **Nachman** with (31) baby Jack on Nachman's lap, (21) Morris/Micky (Hershel & Dasha's), (22) Nick (David & Chane-Fagel's), (23) **Harry/Hershel**.

❧ Top row, left to right: (24) Esther (Sandberg - David & Chane-Fagel's), (25) A. J., (26) **Esther**, (27) **Michel**, (28) Temel, (29) Yossel/Joe (Korman, nephew of Shlaime and Soreh, brother of Temel), (30) Jack (Hershel & Dasha's).

❧ Missing children: **Sam** (passed away Oct 21, 1928 at the age of 24 in a car accident), **Aaron** and his wife Mary from New York, and **Esser** and his wife Bella from Timmins.

Kormans all — from left: Henry, Temel, Isaac, Michel, Fanny, 1945.

Some Korman and Miller Family History
by Esther (Korman) Verred and Jerry Korman

TEMEL AND MICHEL KORMAN were both born in Horodyshche, Minsk Gubernia (now Belarus) and arrived in Rouyn–Noranda with their eldest child, Isaac, in the early 1920s. They lived at 17 – 8th Street. Michel was the head of the building committee that was responsible for the erection of the new shul. His name is on the building cornerstone with the date of the celebration. Temel spent a lot of her time at the Stock Market in Rouyn where she would sit with her cronies and watch the ticker tape. (There was high interest in the stock market because Rouyn–Noranda was a mining town.) Their house was a gathering place for family, friends and the Jewish business travellers who would come up to the North. Temel always had her delicious food at the ready for anyone who dropped

Clockwise from left: Isaac Korman, Temel & Michel Korman, Henry Korman, Fanny Korman, Soreh Korman, ca 1945.

Left to right: Goldie & I.J. Miller, Rose Miller, Noranda, 1944.

by, and Michel was always ready for a *l'chaim* with the Seagrams V.O. and a yahrzeit glass. They kept a strict kosher kitchen (as most people did) with dishes for *milchik* and *fleishik* (milk and meat), and joined in with the community's regular kosher meat orders from Toronto.

They had two more children in Noranda, Henry and Fanny. Henry moved to Montreal and studied medicine at McGill University and Harvard before becoming a surgeon. He married Evelyn and had two children, David and Michael. Fanny and her husband, Eddie Weinstein lived in Rouyn–Noranda for a number of years and then moved to North Bay in 1953 to open a men's wear store. She later moved to Montreal. They had two children, Jack and Maury. In the mid-1960s Temel and Michel sold their house and moved to Montreal.

Isaac Korman was one year old when his parents brought him

Rose Miller & Isaac Korman were married in Noranda in 1945. Above, their ketubah; below, copy of the Quebec marriage record.

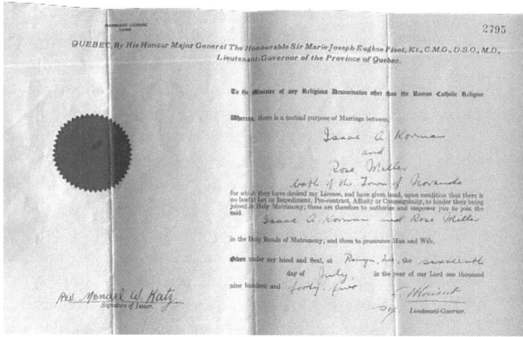

to Noranda. Rose Miller, his future wife, was born in Fort Frances, Ontario, and her family moved from Montreal to Noranda about 1936. Isaac and Rose were high school sweethearts.

After school Isaac enlisted in the Royal Canadian Air Force, and after training was shipped overseas. As a rear gunner–navigator–bombardier in England's Royal Air Force, he was awarded the Distinguished Flying Cross for completing an amazing fifty-seven night missions over Europe. He returned from the war on January 5, 1945.

Rose worked in the family business, Miller's Store on Main Street in Rouyn. She and Isaac married in 1945 in the Noranda Theatre. Isaac ran Mike Korman's Men's Wear on 113 Main Street in Rouyn. We (Jerry and Esther) are their two children. Both of us grew up in Noranda. We lived at 8 – 9th Street in Noranda (two doors away from the shul) until 1957 and then moved to 116 – 18th Street in what was called the New Townsite. When we finished high school we left for university at McGill in Montreal.

As mentioned, Goldie and I. J. Miller (Rose's parents) arrived in Noranda about 1936. They lived in a fourplex at 5 – 7th Street in an upstairs apartment which they rented from Sonya and Nachman Korman. They opened Miller's Store in Rouyn, which sold women's and children's wear.

Goldie was an amazing woman for the time, with one foot in the traditional world and one foot in the modern world. She drove her own car, and was known as an excellent businesswoman. She spoke fluent Ukrainian and other Slavic

Goldie & I.J. Miller with Esther Korman, ca 1954.

A wedding of wide interest took place in Noranda Sunday when Rose Miller, second daughter of Mr. and Mrs. I. J. Miller, became the bride of F-O Isaac Korman, R.C.A.F., P.O.C., a son of Mr. and Mrs. M. man.

The marriage was solemnized on the stage of the Noranda Theatre by Rabbi B. Mednick of Montreal, assisted by Rev. Rabinovich of Kirkland Lake and Rev. W. M. Katz of Noranda, and was according to the Hebrew ritual. After the Rabbi and his assistants had taken their places beneath the canopy on the stage, the bridal party made its way down the aisle in a dignified and colorful procession to the stage.

Nicely spaced, the various groups walked in the following order: the five bridesmaids in floor-length pink dresses, tulle headdresses of pink, and carrying Colonial bouquets, with the five ushers in full dress suits; the best man, the junior bridesmaid, who was demure and pretty in a long dress of pink point d'esprit, and head-dress of same. She was Miss Arlene Miller, younger sister of the bride, and she carried with a bow of yellow tulle the prayer-book, which she presented to the Rabbi when she reached the stage. Following her were the two grandmothers—the groom's, Mrs Sara Korman, of Val d'Or, in a long heliotrope dress, and the bride's, Mrs. E. Wiener, of Montreal, wearing a black dress. Both had corsages roses. Three sweet little flower , Fay and Marcia Sandberg in long Empire style pink silk dresses, and Shirley Rice in white, carried baskets of flowers. The bridegroom walked with his mother, and the bride's mother with the groom's father. Both mothers wore floor-length fitted light blue dresses, fuchsia elbow-length gloves, and fuchsia small hats with veils. Their corsages were of roses. Following her matron of honor, her sister, Mrs. Harry Cohen, who was in a long dress of aqua blue, the bride on the arm of her father was last. She was charming in a long white net gown with fitted basque, and a short veil fell from a bridal coronet, covering her face before her marriage. On reaching the stage she took her place beside the groom, facing the Rabbi, beneath the red c... ... ... with streamers.

The Hebrew contract was read by Rev. Katz in Hebrew and translated in English by Rabbi Mednick, who ... ... translated the blessings which were first chanted in Hebrew. The matron of honor lifted the ... from the bride's face, the ceremonial wine was drunk, and the glass broken. Mrs. Ed. Rice and Miss Olga Skorapad played violin accompanied at the piano by Howard Gegear. For the pro... ... and from the stage they played the Lohengrin "Bridal Chor... Mendelssohn's "Wedding ... Myer Shorony sang, "O ... Me", accompanied by the violins and piano.

Following the marriage ceremony the bridal party, with about three hundred guests, enjoyed a wedding banquet and reception at the Community hall, and dancing after.

On the bride's table was the lovely three-tiered wedding cake decorated with a miniature bridal couple on top and silver leaves and beads. Red candles in silver candelabra were placed on either side of the cake.

M. J. Garmaise was master of ceremonies, and welcomed, on behalf of the bride and the groom, all the guests, especially those who had travelled far to attend, and the grandmothers of the bridal couple. David Miller, of Montreal, uncle of the bride, wished her and her new husband happiness. He also entertained with a Jewish song, "The Cantor on the Sabbath", and for an encore, the Volga Boatmen, with the guests joining in the chorus. Myer Shoroni also favored with some Jewish songs. Rev. Rabinovitch of Kirkland Lake spoke at length in Hebrew, with an inspiring message of hope to all his people. David Korman also had a message, and Rabbi Mednick, a brother of Joe and Sam Mednick of Noranda, wished everyone peace and happiness and comfort. He was pleased to see so many Gentiles present, and would like to see all peoples united as one big family. Rev. Katz led in saying grace after the dinner. The last speakers were the fathers of the bride and groom, and the meal ended with a toast to the happy couple, and the singing in unison, led by Mr. Shorony, of the Hatikvoh, and the national anthem. For dancing the Merrymakers' Orchestra furnished the music. Following a wedding trip to Montreal and the Laurentians, Mr. and Mrs. Isaac Korman will reside at 12 Ninth St., Noranda.

The bridesmaids were Miss Hinda Abrams, of Kirkland Lake, Miss Clare Korman, Timmins, Miss Sophie Korman, Val d'Or, Miss Evelyne Miller, of Montreal, cousin of the bride, and Miss Fanny Korman, sister of the groom. The ushers were Morris Miller, brother of the bride, Nick Korman, Englehart, Moishe Korman, Timmins, Billy Korman, cousin of the groom, and Eddie Weinstein, Montreal, fiance of the groom's sister. Henry Korman, brother of the groom, was best man.

Among the out-of-town guests were Mrs. E. Wiener and her daughter from Montreal, grandmother and aunt of the bride; Mr. and Mrs.

A thorough description of the 1945 marriage of Isaac Korman and Rose Miller appeared in the Rouyn–Noranda Press. The couple were married on the stage of the Noranda Theatre.

D. Miller and daughter Evelyne, Mr. and Mrs. Harry Cohen, brother-in-law and sister of the bride, Mrs. Lillian Neidik, all from Montreal. Rabbi B. Mednick was from Quebec city. From Detroit were Mr. and Mrs. M. Balk, Mrs. N. Talcowsky and Mr. S. Korman; from Toronto, Mr. Harry Korman, Mr. Percy Rightapple, Mr. Sam Fine; from Timmins, Mr. and Mrs. E. Korman, Mr. Carl Horwitz, Mrs. S. Dolfman; from Kirkland Lake Mr. and Mrs. S. Davis, Mr. and Mr. I. Korman and Mr. Mallin, and Mr. S. Schlein, Mr. and Mrs. D. Friedman, Mr. and Mrs. Ben Portnoy; from Englehart, Mr. and Mrs. D. K. Shilling, Mr. and Mrs. Brody, Mrs. S. Steinman; from Val d'Or, Mr. and Mrs. J. Korman, Mr. and Mrs. M. Cartman, Mr. and Mrs. Syd Weinberg; from Duparquet, Mr. and Mrs. Hager; and from Ansonville, Mrs. Sara Crotin, and aunt of the groom, and his cousin, Miss F. Crotin. The bride and groom were recipients of very many lovely and useful wedding gifts.

ENGAGEMENTS

Mr. and Mrs. I. J. Miller, of Noranda, announce the engagement of their daughter, Rose, to Pilot Officer Isaac Korman, D.F. C., R.C.A.F., son of Mr. and Mrs. Michael Korman, of Noranda, who recently returned from overseas.

Marriage announcement, Canadian Jewish Review, March 9, 1945.

languages and the store was a favourite shopping spot for many post–WWII immigrants who could open an account and pay when they could.

The Millers had a cottage on Lake Dufault to which the entire Jewish community of Rouyn–Noranda had an open invitation. Everyone has fond memories of that cottage on Wednesday afternoons and Sundays when the stores were closed.

Rose was the fifth of their six children. Ultimately three children moved to Montreal (Tillie, Morris, and Arlene) and three stayed in Noranda (Ben, Harry, Rose) where they ran Miller's Store with Goldie.

As mentioned, we lived two houses away from the shul. Next door to us lived Becky and Jack Ritter. Jack was a good fishing and curling buddy of our father, Isaac. The Ritters were the first people we remember who got a television set. We were occasionally invited to watch *The Ed Sullivan Show* on CFCL Timmins on Sunday nights. The black and white picture was mostly snow and we tried to discern the people on the screen.

Noranda Curling Club foursome.

Left to right: Isaac Korman, unknown, unknown, Jack Ritter.

Directly across the street from the shul lived Rae and Eddie Rice. Rae was a very talented musician and knitter-crocheter, and was active in Brownies, the IODE and the hospital auxiliary. Eddie owned a bowling alley in Rouyn.

Behind the shul, across the lane at 17 – 8th Street, lived our grandparents, Michel and Temel Korman. In the back of their fourplex on the ground floor lived Pearl and Al Deuitch. Pearl was originally a Fried. Continuing up the lane to 7th Street, our Miller grandparents (Goldie & I.J.) lived in an upstairs apartment in the fourplex; Sonya and Nachman Korman lived downstairs.

MAP *of the* TOWNSITE *of* NORANDA

This development plan was implemented when Noranda got incorporated as a municipality in March 1926. It was put into place so that the city could develop according to the company's will and in a timely manner.

Continuing up the lane to 6th Street, Sam and Zelda Mednick lived at 14 – 6th Street. After the Mednick family moved to Toronto, Sonya and Max Garmaise moved into that house. Max was one of the local judges. He regularly played bridge in a foursome with our father Isaac, Jack Ritter and Max Martin. The Garmaises had three children, Tanya, Mona and David.

Continuing up the lane to 5th Street, Harry and Toby Ironstone had their home at the corner of 5th and Tremoy Road. Harry Ironstone was a local dentist.

On the corner of 6th Street and First Avenue, Esther and Sidney Sandberg lived in a fourplex which they owned. Sidney had a meanswear store on Main Street in Rouyn which later became Martin's Menswear. They had two daughters, Faye and Marsha. Esther was the daughter of David Korman from Englehart.

Esther and Max Martin lived above the Sandbergs with their children, Howard and Sandra. Max Martin had a men's wear store on Main Street in Rouyn.

In the duplex next to the Sandbergs, and also owned by the Sandbergs, Ethel and Sam Korman lived with their children Kathy, Harvey and Sidney. Sam managed the Famous Player theatres in Rouyn–Noranda. §

Group photograph from Joe and Shaindel Korman's 50th Anniversary celebration, Rouyn–Noranda, 1949. Left to right:

❧ Front row seated: Joe Mednick, Rae Mednick, Sarah Isenberg, Shaindel Korman, Joe Korman, Zelda Mednick, Norma Scott.

❧ Standing middle row: Pearl Fried, Goldie Miller, I. J. Miller, Albert Isenberg, Rose Korman, Isaac Korman, unknown, Temel Korman, Gitel Fried, Bella Kravitz, Lazar Kitty, Mike (Motel) Smith, Sam Mednick, unknown, Nathan Wiesenthal, Molly Wiesenthal, Louis Scott.

❧ Back row (standing): Simcha Korman, Osher Bloom, Michel Korman.

Joe & Shaindel Korman, and Chaskel & Doreen Korman
by Doreen (Shub) Korman (daughter-in-law)

ACCORDING TO THEIR PASSPORTS, Shaindel and Joseph Korman became naturalized Canadian citizens on September 18, 1929.

Joseph was shown as a merchant, born in 1885 in Horodyshche, Minsk Gubernia (now Belarus). Shaindel was born in Smorodzk in the Stolin district of Ukraine.

Chaskel Bernstein, whom Joseph adopted into his family, arrived in Canada in August 1948. Preceding his arrival, there were articles in the newspaper reporting on the arrival of a Jewish youth who had been decorated by both the Polish and Czech governments. The boat he was on was the *Aquitania* and most of the passengers were reportedly orphans from Europe. There was another girl that Joe wanted to adopt, but she declined. We did meet up with her in Toronto many years later; Chaskel accidentally met her at Kensington Market where she had a store.

In 1948 Joe was operating a grocery store. Chaskel worked in it when he was not in school. Joe also started prospecting for gold and bought several shares in gold mines. He also had Chaskel accompany him on these prospecting expeditions. Over time Joe also acquired several properties consisting of a bowling alley, commercial buildings, and residential homes. Then he acquired the infamous Radio Hotel and attached apartments. The Radio Hotel had live performers on a weekly basis through the accommodation of a talent scout by the name of Harold Kudlats. (Upon our joining Temple Anshe Shalom in Hamilton in the

fice: Warwick Hotel, Toronto.

KORMAN, Joseph Yosef, Hotel Executive. Born 6 Jan 1885, Russia, son of Sora and Shloma Korman. Married Shaindel Korman, active, Sisterhood; Hadassah; Faiga Korman Chapter; named in honour of her sister. Business: Owner and operator, Radio Hotel and Miss Rouyn Steak House. Affiliations: General Israel Orphans Home; Special Emergency Food Committee; Hachnuses Kalo; Hebrew National Association, Folks Farein-Hachnuses Orchem; one of the founders; Knesset Israel Congregation; Board, Rabbinical College of Canada; Zionist Organization of Canada; Quebec Hotels Association; Quebec Restaurants Association; Nun's Association;

J. Y. KORMAN

Rouyn Chamber of Commerce; Ner Israel Rabbinical College; Canadian Corps; active, State of Israel Bonds. Came to Canada in 1921, with his parents, settling in Engelhart, Ontario; and worked on the Northern Ontario Railroad Expansion Program, before moving on to Ansonville, Ontario, where he went into dairying. In 1927, moved to Rouyn, Quebec; built the first private enterprise on the Noranda Mines Property, and was the first to establish a retail grocery store in Rouyn. Rel Affil: Knesset Israel and Agudath Israel Anshei Sfard, Toronto. Res: 134 Carter Ave. Office: Radio Hotel, Rouyn.

From "Who's Who in Canadian Jewry," 1963.

early 1970s, we found that Harold and his family were also members.)

Chaskel was a self-taught musician; he played the trumpet and accordion. He never did play at his father's hotel but did at other local hotels. Chaskel became the adoring adult "child" that the Kormans had longed for, and he was eternally grateful and loyal to the family as if he had been born a Korman.

In 1949, Joe and Shaindel celebrated their fiftieth anniversary and their joy of having Chaskel in their lives by ordering a Torah scroll from somewhere in Europe.

Joe also facilitated bringing Chaskel's only living family to Canada. Chaskel's birth sister, Natasha Adamek, along with her husband and infant daughter, immigrated to Canada in 1949.

JOE KORMAN PASSED away in 1963. On August 31, 1964, the day of the unveiling at Dawes Road cemetery in Toronto, Rabbi Monson thought Chaskel should meet a Jewish girl, so Marsha Sandberg–Feldman (my cousin through marriage) set up a "coffee date" for Chaskel with me, Doreen Shub, from Timmins. We married on February 22, 1965 — the rest is history.

After Joe Korman's death, Chaskel had been left with his estate, which consisted of several homes, a bowling alley, buildings and most notably the Radio Hotel. By the end of 1964 Chaskel had sold the hotel and he felt there was no further need to continue with the thought of living there.

After we returned from our honeymoon, we decided to live in Montreal because Chaskel still had property there. Now he needed a "job" for an income. He worked for his brother-in-law, Victor Adamak, in his business.

In the fall of 1966, Shaindel moved to Montreal and resided temporarily with us in Chomedey. The purpose of the move was to have her in a position to be accepted to a new Jewish nursing home in Cote St Luc, Maimonides. It wasn't until the following spring that Shaindel was admitted to this facility.

After the Noranda synagogue closed, the Torahs were given back to the families who had donated them. Upon Shaindel moving to Chomedy, the Noranda Torah was moved with her. Shaindel Korman passed away in April 1969.

OUR DAUGHTER, Serena Miriam, was born in June 1966 and our son Samuel Joseph "Joey" (named for Chaskel and Joe Korman) was born in May 1969. That September, we moved to Toronto, part of the exodus of English-speaking Quebecers who left due to political reasons. Chaskel started up a new business, introducing central vacuum systems into the area.

In 1971, wanting and missing the small-town life, we relocated to Burlington, still within an easy drive to Toronto. We joined the Burlington Jewish community and the children participated. Chaskel always enjoyed boating and we as a family continued to do so for many years. We went from his fourteen-foot Brunswick boat to a thirty-six-foot Chris Craft and we were able to spend many enjoyable years on Lake Ontario in our floating cottage.

We joined the Oakville shul on Morrison Drive and temporarily placed the Torah on loan to them. In the mid-1970s we realized the children's Jewish education would suffer unless we moved to a larger Jewish congregation. After much deliberation, we joined Temple Anshe Sholom in Hamilton.

In 1982, Doreen permanently removed the Torah from Oakville to Hamilton for Joey's bar mitzvah. Several years later the Torah was donated to Anshe Sholom. It is the only Torah in the congregation that can be traced back to a donor and is still marked and referred to as "the Korman Torah."

Chaskel Korman passed away from Parkinsons and complications on October 22, 2012. On January 27, 2020, our daughter, Serena Korman, passed away from juvenile diabetes and complications. §

Chaskel (Harry) with Joe & Shaindel, Rouyn–Noranda, 1950

Eulogy for Chaskel (Harry) Korman
By David Halporn

The following poetic words were delivered by David Halporn, a grand-nephew, at Chaskel's funeral in Hamilton on October 24, 2012:

FROM Wordsworth's ode *Intimations of Immortality*, from "Recollections of Early Childhood":

> The Moon doth with delight
> Look around her when the heavens are bare;
> Waters on a starry night
> Are beautiful and fair;
> The sunshine is a glorious birth;
> But yet I know, where'er I Go,
> That there hath past away a glory from the earth.

Harry Korman: There hath passed away a glory from the earth. This glorious, adored man, friend, beloved member of the Korman clan, Shriner, favourite cousin, in-law to the Shubs, godfather. Proud member of this congregation. Zaida Pops. And, of course, loving husband to Doreen for nearly half a century.

To me and my family, he was Uncle Harry. He was actually

my great-uncle, and if any uncle deserved that moniker, it was surely him. Who was this great man and where did he come from? Probably everyone in this room, with the exception of my mother Nadi, knew Harry only from his second life, his life in Canada. We knew the man with the irrepressible smile, the sparkling eyes, the man who, when he embraced you, kissed and hugged you with his entire heart, the optimist, the man who always put others at ease, the one who was full of life, the generous one, the pourer of stiff drinks, the sharp dresser, the maker of the best hamburgers, the dog lover.

But in his first life, in Eastern Europe, he was Chaskel. Brother to Natasha. Son of Sally and Sam Bernstein. He was Eulich and nicknamed Adjoo. *School-boy with his satchel / And shining morning face.* He studied Hebrew. Stood below the counter of his father's butcher shop while his mother fed him treats. Played soccer and led a normal kid's life.

Then, suddenly, his home was in occupied territory. The Soviet army, the German army. He and his family were moved into a ghetto. Then he was alone. He was a dweller of the Polish forest, a twelve-year-old Partisan spy. Lieutenant of the Czech army. Then a decorated war hero. Student in Prague. Player of the accordion he had captured from a German soldier who was likely a decade or more older than him.

AFTER HE CROSSED the ocean, he became Harry, son of Joe and Shaindel, high school student in Noranda. Driver of fast cars, striking young adult, business owner. Captain of his boat. Great father and grandfather.

Who among us, knowing this happy, content, life-filled man, would have guessed he emerged from anywhere other than the most carefree of childhoods and the warm embrace an adoring, loving family. Surely such warmth marked his earliest time on this earth, before all the terrible loss, and how I wish we had stories and images of the joyful boyhood. If we did, I think we would find a close version of the boy Wordsworth wrote of:

> Behold the Child among his new born blisses,
> A six years Darling of a pigmy size!
> See, where mid work of his own hand he lies,
> Fretted by sallies of his mother's kisses,
> With light upon him from his father's eyes.
> See, at his feet, some little plan or chart,
> Some fragment from his dream of human life . . .

But as we know, Harry stopped receiving Sally's kisses so very early on, as the great events of 1930s and 1940s in Europe swept his family life away like flotsam in a tidal wave. Whatever may have been in that six-year-old's fragment of a dream of human life, it did not include separation from his mother, did not include seeing, at the age of nine, his father shot down in the street, did not include entrusting his life to and living among strangers. It would not have included learning how to handle a gun before he learned to drive a car. To spy behind enemy lines. To lose, before boyhood was barely over, almost everything he had known and had ever given him comfort.

And yet, out of all that misery and tragedy — darker than most of us have ever known or can imagine — out of all that emerged this shining gem of a man called Harry.

How can we explain this? That our Harry came out of that black hole not bitter and hardened, but hopeful and tender and kind. Ready to love and be loved (and everybody loved Harry, didn't they?) That was his spark and the tragedies of his youth simply could not put it out.

Chaskel (Harry) Korman (front) with Murray Rice (left) and other band members playing at a local hotel, Rouyn.

Though the radiance which was once so bright
Be now for ever taken from my sight,
Though nothing can bring back the hour
Of splendour in the grass, of glory in the flower;
We will grieve not, rather find
Strength in what remains behind.

That was the boy of Wordsworth's ode, who lost his youth to the ordinary cruelties of merely growing up. Our Harry lost his youth to extraordinary cruelties, but he decided no less than the other young man: *I will grieve not, rather find / Strength in what remains behind.* And what strength he found. And what amazing things he did with it.

To paraphrase one of the world's *other* great optimists, Robert Kennedy: Some believe there is nothing one man or one woman can do against the enormous array of the world's ills — against misery, against ignorance, or injustice and violence. Yet many of the world's great movements, of thought and action, have flowed from the work of a single man. These men moved the world, and so can we all. Each of us can work to change a small portion of events, and in the total of all these acts will be written history.

My Uncle Harry was one of those men who wrote history. By standing strong, as a mere child, against an evil that tried to end him and an entire people, he helped write one of the defining stories of the twentieth century.

Harry crossed an ocean and embraced the chance to live out a life of purpose and happiness in this place. He chose adventure. He chose a new, fresh world that matched his temperament, his imagination, and his optimism. In so doing, Harry set in motion that small portion of events that quite literally created us. If he had not settled in Canada, my grandparents would have had no particular reason to come here, my mother would have not met my father, Harry would not have met Doreen, they would not have shared their beautiful forty-seven years. I would not be here; Tamara would not be here; Joey, Serena, Aaron, Sarah, Sam, Natasha. We descendants of Sam and Sally — all this love would not exist.

So, today, as we send you to your rest, we thank you Harry, for your role in our history, for creating us. Against every possible odd, you chose hope over despair in your dream of human life.

I say to my Aunt Doreen and my cousins, Serena and Joey, and their families: you have the Kormans and the Shubs, and they are big clans and you are lucky. Lean on them, mourn with them today and in the days to come.

But our little branch, the one that traces itself to the Bernsteins, we were already so small and today it feels like we are so very much smaller. As we each move forward with our personal, private loss, let us not forget that Harry has given us each other and in so doing has given us something bigger than ourselves. Our family is both small and immense. Let us hold it close, and Harry will be with us always.

Harry will also be with us whenever we might step out into a dark night and see *the Moon with delight / Look around her when the heavens are bare.* For my part, when I look at a full moon, I will remember that as a boy Harry had to hide in the forest where the bright moonlight meant that he could be discovered and killed that much more easily. We can simply bask in its glow and admire its beauty. That is his gift to us. You were one man, Harry, you changed a small portion of events. And for us, you changed the world. §

My Sixteen Years in the North
by Harvey Philip Korman

David Korman in Englehart, Ontario, 1920 (OJA)

I WAS BORN at the Youville Hospital in Noranda on October 19, 1948. That makes me an Israeli birthyear child. There were only a very few Jewish kids born in Rouyn–Noranda after me. Rae and Eddie Rice were the last Jews living there, except for occasional Jewish men who were involved in the mining industry. The second-last Jewish resident was Rose Korman.

Our family's first attempt to get out of Rouyn–Noranda was a move to Downsview (Toronto), when I was in grade five, to start the school year. That did not last long as by October we were back in Rouyn–Noranda. The second attempt was when I was in grade eight. We moved to Kirkland Lake after the start of the school year. My grandfather had built the first fully automated bowling alley in Kirkland Lake and my father was needed to run the business. After a month we were back in Rouyn–Noranda.

My father wanted to bring his family out of Quebec not only because we were Jewish, but because we were English. It was getting to be more of a challenge to live and do business in English in Quebec. My family's final move to Toronto was in 1965. So I lived in Noranda for just over sixteen years.

My grandfather, David Korman, was the first in his family to come to Canada; according to family lore, he ended up in Englehart, Ontario, in the early 1900s "because that was the end of the railway line at the time." He knew the North, with the new mines opening,

Sam Korman's family owned and operated the Capitol and
Paramount Theatres in Rouyn and the Noranda Theatre
in Noranda. At left, Harvey Korman in usher's uniform.

offered many business opportunities. He and my grandmother,
Chane-Fagel, had four children, Golda, Samuel, Esther and Daniel,
all born in Englehart.

My grandfather led the way for his parents (my great-
grandparents, Shlaime and Soreh) and his eight brothers and one sister
to come to Canada and escape all the horror that was about to unfold
to the Jewish people of Europe. They settled in Rouyn–Noranda and
Val d'Or in Quebec, and Englehart, Kirkland Lake, Haileybury and
Timmins in Ontario. Since he had lots of siblings and they had lots
of children, it seems that I was related to more than half the Jewish

NATION-WIDE CONCERN OPERATES NEW THEATRE

Left: Sam Korman's birth record, Englehart, 1907. Right: Newspaper story about Sam Korman, 1938.

SAM KORMAN
Enterprising Manager of the Capito and Noranda Theatres.

SAM KORMAN IS MANAGER

Made His Debut in the Show Busi-nes at Twelve Years of Age in Englehart

Sam Korman, enterprising man-ager of the Noranda and Capitol Theatres here, though comparatively young in years, has had a long and thorough training in the theatre bus-iness, and is well qualified to look after the interests of the two modern movie houses in Rouyn and Noranda of which he has charge.

Mr. Korman was born in Engle-hart just thirty-one years ago, and made his debut in the business of conducting a theatre when he was only twelve years of age, starting in at the Palace Theatre in Engle-hart, which was operated by his father, Mr. David Korman. Six years later, then only eighteen years of age, Sam Korman was manager of the Broadway theatre in Haileybury. When his father purchased the Clas-sic Theatre in Cobalt in 1937, Sam took over the managing of, and conducted the theatre successfully until it was sold to Allen Brothers in 1930.

Following the sale of the Cobalt theatre Mr. Korman temporarily forsook the show business, and for five years carried on a real estate business in Kirkland Lake. Then in September of last year, when his father became associated with Fa-mous Players Canadian Corporation in the operation of the Noranda Theatre, he came here as manager.

Since that time Mr. Korman has been among the busiest men in the twin cities. Re-adjustment, re-dec-oration and other changes at the Noranda Theatre following the change of management occupied much of his time, and in addition the work was then just getting well under way at the Capitol Theatre in Rouyn, giving him added duties and responsibilities.

Mr. Korman feels, however, that the result was worth the effort, and is confident that the residents of the two towns will be more than satis-fied with the entertainment offered by the two theatres.

population living in the North.

My grandfather was mayor of Englehart for many terms, and after him my uncle was also mayor of Englehart, also for many terms.

My father, Sam Korman, was sent to Noranda to manage the family movie theatre business in a time when there was no TV. His family opened theatres in Cobalt, Haileybury, Englehart, Noranda (the Noranda Theatre) and Rouyn (Capitol and Paramount theatres; the Paramount was a French theatre) in partnership with Famous Players. All the theatres were operating before I was born.

My father also invested in commercial real estate and mortgages in Noranda. He had the Woolworth block in Noranda in partnership with

Marriage of Samuel Korman
& Ethel Abel, Noranda, 1946.

his brother and the Quebec Hydro building in partnership with his brother and uncle, Michel Korman.

When our family moved to Toronto, my father commuted between Rouyn–Noranda (to look after his business interests) and Toronto. He passed on January 23, 1973 while in Noranda. Isaac Korman went looking for him when he did not show up for their morning coffee and found him in his hotel room. I was in Sault Ste Marie, Michigan, with the Lakehead University varsity hockey team. I had been called up from the development team and did not tell my family. I was rooming with other members of the team and we let a friend stay in our house to use our colour TV. He answered my sister Kathy's call and told her I was in Sault Ste Marie. My sister called the radio station and they told her which hotel the team was staying at and she was able to contact me after our Friday night game. My father's

The Noranda St. Pats hockey team during the 1963/64 season. Harvey Korman appears in the middle row, wearing sweater number 5.

ﻼ Front row: Bob Pate (left), Bill Serediak, Bill Furlong (manager), Jacques Ross, Gerry Fassett. ﻼ Middle row: Mr. Bouchard, Paul Lessard, Ghislain Arsenault, Harvey Korman, Jacques Parent, Rene Quesnel, unknown, Chesty Clowater (coach). ﻼ Back row: Marcel Vanier (left), Maurice St. Jacques, Denis Beaule, Dale Tallon, Jean Martin, Jean Pierre Bordeleau.

uncle, Michel Korman, stayed with him as the *shomer* (watchman) overnight and accompanied him in the hearse to Toronto. I flew home Saturday morning for the funeral. My father and mother are laid to rest in the Palmerston section of Dawes Road Jewish Cemetery (Toronto) with a lot of other family members who lived up north.

There was a tragic fire in a movie theatre in Montreal in which many kids perished. Afterwards, the province passed a law that children sixteen and under could only attend a movie theatre on a Saturday matinee. The restriction lasted more than thirty years. On days other than a Saturday, I was able to watch movies in the theatre's projection booth or I would sit near the front row and if the police checked the theatre for kids, I would crawl under the seats and run into the back room. I shared a lot of this experience with my cousin Jerry Korman. Luckily, I was never caught. Another advantage of having a father run a movie theatre was to get large paper bags filled with fresh popcorn.

In the years just before we moved to Toronto, Quebec passed laws limiting only one new English movie release for the entire province. Naturally, Montreal got it first. My father had to smuggle English movies across the border and pay the fines.

Kathy
Korman

My father met my mother, Ethel Abel, in Toronto in the mid-1940s. They were married in Noranda. My mother was born in Canada and grew up in small towns too: the towns of Southampton and nearby Port Elgin, Ontario, on the shore of Lake Huron. Their Port Elgin house is designated a heritage home. Her father, a fur trapper, emigrated to Canada from Hungary about 1909. My parents had three children — my sister Kathryn (Edery), then me, then my brother Sidney.

My sister has a picture of my father in his army uniform. All we know is that he enlisted in the army, but the war ended before he could be shipped out. He never talked about his army experience.

When I was four or five, I had a life-endangering experience on the street in front of our house. It was spring and the water from the melting snow had flooded the street and the ice had blocked the water from draining down the storm sewer. The town had lifted the sewer cover to allow the water and ice to drain. There was a huge snow bank next to the sewer, the weather was warmer, and we were playing in the water and on the snow bank. Somehow, I slid on the ice and ended up on top of the open sewer. My feet were in the hole and the only thing stopping me from being swallowed up was my ability to hold on to the snow bank. I was screaming and all the kids thought it was a joke. Luckily Mike (Motel) Smith, who was coming home from work, heard my screams and pulled me out of trouble.

My mother maintained a kosher house and kept the Jewish traditions alive. She made many traditional Jewish foods such as challah, bagels, hamantashen, gefilte fish, dill pickles, sauerkraut, chicken soup with matzah balls, brisket, kugel, latkes, horse radish with red beets, chopped liver, blintzes, cabbage rolls (holiskes) and pastries. I helped with the grinding to make the chopped liver, gefilte fish, horse radish and sauerkraut.

Celebrating Jewish holidays like Passover was challenging for kids as there was no kosher-for-Passover junk food. Chocolate matzah brought in from Toronto was our special treat. We celebrated with pizza after Passover.

Keeping kosher in Noranda also presented challenges for me, especially when I participated in overnight hockey trips and out-of-town tournaments. The biggest challenge was when I travelled to Quebec City for the seventh annual Pee Wee hockey tournament (for thirteen-year-olds), with the Noranda Pee Wee all-star team. Because we made it to the finals, we were there for one week. I stayed kosher the whole time. It was a difficult feat for me.

We lost in the finals to Drummondville in front of 13,000 fans cheering for Drummondville, a local team. Our team was a great team, with two future NHL stars on it. All the members of that all-star team were given a junior membership at the Noranda Golf Club, which normally did not welcome Jews as members. I remember my father commenting that I slipped through the cracks.

My father's sister, Esther Sandberg, lived in the fourplex next to us. Her husband, Sidney Sandberg, built it and the duplex we lived in. My father was very close and supportive to his sister. Sidney passed when I was very young, but I was old enough to remember him. Esther and Sidney had two daughters, Marsha and Faye. My father spent a lot of time at his sister's place. I loved going there with him because my Aunt Esther always gave me treats.

B'nai Brith, Northern Ontario region meeting, Kirkland Lake, 1940s.

❧ Front row, left to right: Sol Shankman (Timmins), Harry Miller (Rouyn–Noranda), Montague Raisman (Toronto), Saul Ross (Kirkland Lake), M. Brown (North Bay), Rev. Rabinovitch (KL).

❧ Second row: Sam Langer (KL), Isaac Korman (R–N), L. Revzen (R–N), Norman Koza (Timmins), Jack Halpert (Timmins), Manny Abrams (Timmins), M. Kaplan (KL), Sam Finkleman (KL).

❧ Third row (all KL): Phil Mervin, [unidentified], Jack Kussner, Sam Davis, Harry Moscoe, Don Wertman, Max Levine, Joe Scott, Irving Kokotow.

❧ Back row (all KL): Abe Ginsberg, William Berk, Al Brown.

My father also spent a lot of time at the home of his uncle and aunt, Michel and Temel Korman, on 17 – 8th Street. Temel was a great cook and smoker and was known to drop her cigarette ashes occasionally into her soup with a whoop.

Everyone loved to party and drink. Liquor at celebrations was not safe. But then, in Quebec the liquor laws were much different than the rest of the country. The drinking age was lower than Ontario, and you could buy beer at grocery stores. In fact, when my parents left me alone in Noranda, we would order liquor from the grocery store and they would deliver it to our house. We were all underage. No one checked our ID.

The Noranda Jewish community at one time, I was told, had more than forty Jewish families. The synagogue was the focal point of the community. We shared the Jewish holidays and everyone was invited to share in *simchas*. In the community's early years, a *shoichet* (slaughterer) would arrive, paid for by the community. Certified *mohels* (circumciser), such as Rabbi Linder from Timmins, were also called upon for a *bris* (circumcision).

The young Jewish community was very close. We were together for cheder classes, Young Judaea, birthday parties and sleepovers. Birthday parties and sleepovers with non-Jewish kids were rare. For me it gave me an advantage when the milkman, Mr. Kravitz, let me help him deliver the milk in his horse-drawn milk wagon. Another advantage was when our school ran a Betty Crocker promotion, I went to all the Jewish families and my sales volume won me first prize.

As kids we had lots of time to kill (there were no internet, cell phones or video games) and one of the things we did was to publish a local newsletter. Our chief editor was David Garmaise. Headlines were about our dogs and happenings in the Jewish community. Too bad no one saved an edition. David and I were great friends. After Cheder classes, we would go to Kresge's and steal Dinky toys. We built up quite a nice collection until the day my father came home and asked me about taking the toys. The manager at Kresge caught us and knew my father and rather than call the police, he called my father to end the adventures. I gave back all our stash and never to this day took anything from a store again.

At the time we were growing up in Noranda, I remember emissions of sulphur dioxide from the mine would fall on the town. The clouds of toxins made it irritating to breathe and made us choke when we were outside. In addition to sulphur dioxide, today (2023) it is known that for decades the people were overexposed to arsenic, cadmium, nickel and lead.

I was around seven years old when we got English TV. We needed rabbit ears to get reception from the English station coming from Timmins. In the beginning the reception was not very clear. There was a local French station with great reception but we did not speak French. That was, in my opinion, a failure of the English school system and our parents.

In the early 1950s we had operator-assisted phone calls and party lines. I would listen in to the conversations and by removing the mouth piece no one could tell I was on the line.

The city's power grid operated on 25 Hz before the changeover to 60 Hz in the 1950s. When that happened, coincidentally, my future wife's uncle from Toronto came up to Noranda to buy all the 25-cycle machines that were being discarded; he sold them to the mines that were still operating on 25 cycle.

In another coincidence, in a group photo of representatives from various Northern B'nai Brith lodges, taken at a Northern region meeting in Kirkland Lake in the early forties, sitting in the front row, representing B'nai Brith Canada, was my wife's great uncle, Montague Raisman (see page 92).

It was *bashert*, something meant to be or perhaps just fate that my aunt, Esther Sandberg, playing matchmaker, fixed me up with Robin Dalgorf from Toronto, who turned out to be my future wife. We were married on July 25, 1974. We have three kids, Skyler, Shane and Ashley and, so far, five grandchildren. My kids were constantly asked if they were related to the famous children's author, Gordon Korman, to which they were proudly able to answer yes.

Fundraisers for various Jewish causes would come to Noranda to raise money from our parents. The kids had a special Jewish National Fund blue collection box. We filled enough of those boxes to plant hundreds of trees in Israel.

Anyone growing up in Noranda will remember crossing frozen Lake Osisko in the winter as a short cut to Rouyn. Once, while using this route when I was about eleven, I saw in the distance three known trouble makers (because I was Jewish) coming towards me. The path was narrow and the snow off the path was deep. I was determined not to show fear. I was rewarded with snow in the face and being tossed off the path into the deep snow.

For one of my birthdays, one of my invited friends did not come to my birthday. Of course, I was hurt and asked him at school what happened. I will remember his answer forever. He was German and his parents forbade him from attending my birthday party because I was Jewish.

OUR PARENTS TRIED very hard to give us a Jewish education through both cheder and Young Judaea. I was at the synagogue four times a week for cheder classes and once a week for Young Judaea on Sunday mornings. Then we were there for all the *simchas* and Jewish holidays. The community rabbi taught us cheder each day after school from four to six P.M. Other than my siblings, the only other kids at my elementary school who were Jewish were my cousin Esther and, for a while, her brother Jerry. Cheder brought all the Jewish kids together. We learned how to read Hebrew and about Jewish culture. We were also wild and drove our teachers mad. I cannot count how many times I was hit on the back with his wooden ruler. On one occasion the ruler snapped in half and we all broke out into laughter. It was a social time and I looked forward to attending every day.

Pre-cheder was also play time. We would play floor hockey in the basement of the shul. I always made sure there was a rink to play hockey on because I scored a lot of goals. After ringing the bell, the teacher often had to come down and drag us up to class.

Young Judaea grounded us in Jewish culture and history. The older kids would go to Camp Biluim, a leadership training camp, and come

Head table photo shows (from left) Frieda
& David Korman, Harvey Korman, and
Sam & Ethel Korman, 1961.

back to Noranda to teach the
younger children all their new
knowledge. I was part of the
younger group. They taught us
many traditional dances.

All the northern towns
had Young Judaea and once a
year we would have a convention,
bringing all the Jewish kids
together from Noranda, Kirkland
Lake, Timmins, North Bay and
Sudbury. I have fond memories
and a lifelong friend arising from
those conventions.

Our group was invited to perform Israeli dances on the local
television station. The girls wore a navy skirt and a white blouse. The

Mr. and Mrs. Samuel Korman
request the honour of your presence
at the Bar-Mitzvah
of their son
Harvey Philip
on Saturday, the second of September
nineteen hundred and sixty-one
at nine o'clock
Knesseth Israel Congregation
Noranda, Quebec

Luncheon
at the Elisabeth Room
of the Windsor Hotel.

Cocktails and Dinn
Noranda Ho
7 p

guys, black pants and a white shirt. We all had the Young Judaea tie. The dancers were Jerry Korman, Esther Korman, Harvey Korman, Kathryn Korman, Laurie Miller, Bernadine Miller, David Garmaise and our leader, Mona Garmaise. That was an exciting event and I got lots of comments from kids at school saying that they saw us.

My parents also sent us to Jewish summer camps. We were sent for the second term to Camp New Moon (about six years), Camp Shalom (one year) and Camp Hagshama (one year). Before and after camp, we would spend time at our grandfather's cottage on Round Lake, between Englehart and Kirkland Lake, Ontario. The Ironstones, from Noranda, also had a cottage on Round Lake.

As the Jewish community left town, it was more difficult to get a *minyan* and the community improvised. I remember when I was twelve, Chaskel Korman needed a tenth person for *yahrzeit*. He picked me up and put a siddur under my arm to officially count me as the tenth.

I had my bar mitvah in Noranda in 1961. There was a huge reception at the Noranda hotel; the next day the local newspaper ran a story about it with a photo of the head table. My sister clipped out the picture and I still have it today. There were three more bar mitzvahs in Noranda after mine: Joe Miller and Marvin Miller in 1963, and the last one was Malcolm Finkelman on May 15, 1965. Our Hebrew teacher, Meyer Sharony, prepared all of us for our bar mitzvahs. I have an audio tape recording of Mr. Sharony singing my Torah portion.

MY BRIEF YEARS in Noranda seemed packed with activity. At fourteen I was in a rock band called the Wild Cats. We were very fortunate to be able to practice on the stage in the basement of the synagogue. Since most of the band members were under sixteen, we had to hire a driver to get us to our out-of-town gigs. We would come home from these gigs at about five in the morning. My cousin, Jack Weinstein, was the manager for one year, and some of the band members formed close relationships with my cousin Esther (Korman) Verred and Bernadine Miller.

Chaskel Korman, who operated the Radio Hotel in Rouyn, would sneak me in to listen to the rock groups playing in his bar. That was huge for me because I was underage. On my side was that I was tall and looked older. He introduced me to a sax player who gave me a lot of tips when I was first starting up as the sax player in our rock band.

My mother let me play football and hockey; not common for a Jewish kid in Noranda. But if we had a game on Yom Kippur, my mother would say, "If Sandy Koufax can miss the first game in the World Series, you can miss your game on the Jewish holidays too." Players were often targetted for being Jewish. A friend on one of the other Noranda midget teams told me before games they would discuss who to pick on, the French kid or the Jewish kid. There was only one French kid on our team. The French kids were on teams from Rouyn. My advantage was that I was bigger than him and he was an easier target.

Being active in sports and Jewish also made me a target on the school playground and streets. I cannot count how many times I came home with bruises. I was 6'2" and nearly 190 pounds by my bar mitzvah and sometime while growing up I became bigger than most, so the beatings stopped and I got payback with the guys that hurt me the most. Along the way there were rock fights in the lane and snowball fights on the streets. Luckily, we all survived them.

At the Noranda High School, in grades 8 and 9, Mr. Jackson coached me in the discus toss. I came in first place in the regional competition in both years. In my first year at the University of Waterloo, I broke the university record for discus toss.

I was in the co-op program at the UW and chose a job at the Noranda Mines for my work term. I was placed in the machine shop, above ground, for the four months. My father was there, commuting back and forth from Toronto. I later transferred to the Lake Head

Noranda High Boys Track Team
A Noranda newspaper published this photo of Noranda High's track-and-field team after an important meet. "Top star Harvey Korman" is in the front row, third from left.

University in Thunder Bay. I hitchhiked to Toronto and back with a friend one summer to compete in a track and field event. Each of us won our event.

I was sixteen when my family moved to Toronto. My father commuted back and forth because he still had his business in Noranda. But with the rising popularity of television and a dwindling English population, the English theatre in Noranda was not popular any more. The Noranda theatre was the first to close.

Mixing into the Toronto culture was a challenging project for a kid from a small town in northern Quebec. At my first French class, my teacher said that I could never read French in her class again because I had a Quebec accent. Unfortunately, somewhere along the way, I lost my ability to speak French.

In conclusion, growing up Jewish in Noranda was a great experience and it certainly left a huge impression on my life. Recently I told my seven-year-old granddaughter that when I was her age, living in Noranda, we did not have TV, cell phones or video games. When I asked her what she would have done, she said, "I would not have lasted a day." §

Sam & Zelda Mednick (left) with Sonia & Nachman Korman.

Nachman & Sonia Korman in Rouyn–Noranda
by Jean Korman (daughter-in-law)

NACHMAN KORMAN WAS born March 25, 1900 in Stolin, Minsk, according to his naturalization papers issued to him in Timmins, Ontario.

In August 1921, Nachman Korman departed from Warsaw, Poland on the ship *Scandinavian* headed for Canada. The manifest indicates that his port of arrival was Quebec, his birthplace was Russia (Horodyshche to be exact) and his citizenship was Polish. Passage was paid by his brother David residing in Englehart, Ontario. He arrived as a "farmer" and boarded a CPR train to Englehart.

In March 1924, Nachman brought his intended bride Sonia Feldman from Pinsk, Belarus. They were married in Timmins where their first son William was born. They settled in Rouyn–Noranda where they had two more sons, Jack and Saul.

Nachman was first employed in the mine. Later, he owned a grocery store for a few years before opening a retail menswear store in Rouyn called Esquire Menswear.

Shlaime and Soreh Korman, the patriarch and matriarch of the Korman family, had nine sons and one daughter. Several of the children lived in Rouyn–Noranda: Joe, Michel, Nachman and Sam. David lived in Englehart, Esser in Timmins, Harry (Hershel) in Englehart briefly and then Toronto, Itzik in Kirkland Lake, Aaron in

Left, Saul & Myrna Korman. Middle, Jack & Jean Korman. Right, Willie Korman as a newly-graduated M.D. Below, Willie as a bar-mitzvah boy circa 1951.

New York, Esther in Val d'Or and Montreal. The youngest, Sam, was killed in a car accident.

Living in Noranda was not easy. Cold winters were difficult, employment not easy, language a barrier. The community of Jews functioned well. They needed each other, depended on each other, loved one another and were tightly knit.

Nachman and Sonia gave their sons the best education available. Their firstborn, Bill, went on to Montreal and Toronto where he received his MD. Soon after he was accepted in Baltimore, Maryland where he was trained as an obstetrician and gynecologist. He and his wife Sivi had three children, Robert, Alice and Rachel.

Jack, their middle son, took off time from school to help his father in Esquire Menswear during a period when Nachman needed surgery. Jack later built his own successful retail business (Corby's) in Toronto where he resided with his wife Jean (me) and their four children — Debbie, David, Mitchell and Aviva.

Saul, their youngest son, also established a successful retail business (Korry's) in Toronto. He and his wife Myrna had three children — Jodie, Michael and Shawn. §

Dvoshe Korman and her four sons, Rouyn–Noranda circa 1942. Clockwise from upper left: Sonny, Dvoshe, Isaac, Henry, Willie.

Simcha & Dvoshe Korman
by Isaac Korman

*M*Y FATHER, Simcha Korman, was born in Horodyshche, Minsk Gubernia (now in Belarus) and served in the Russian army. My mother, Dvoshe (Slepak) Korman, was from a town about ten kilometres away and my father used to regularly walk over to visit her when they were courting. My parents married two weeks before my father left for Canada in 1925.

My father arrived in Ansonville where he worked in the grocery store belonging to Barney Nosov. He worked there and brought over Dvoshe in 1927. He also brought over his sister, Sorel, who married Walter Crotin and lived in Ansonville.

Simcha and Dvoshe moved to Noranda where his other sister and brother-in-law, Temel and Michel Korman, lived. He opened a second-hand store on Third Avenue, and later moved the store to

Perreault Street in Rouyn. They lived at 125 First Avenue. At the time, phone calls were made through a live Bell operator and their phone number was 478.

Dvoshe was kept busy raising their four sons, Sonny, Isaac, Willie and Henry, but also found time, like most Jewish women in Rouyn–Noranda, to be involved with Hadassah. She regularly helped a neighbouring Ukrainian woman correspond with her family in Ukraine because the woman had difficulty with reading and writing. My mother would read the letters and transcribe her responses in Ukrainian. She was also an excellent cook. I remember once Murray and Stanley Rice came over to eat with us. When they went home, they told their mother, Rae Rice, how much they enjoyed the food. Rae then called my mother to ask what she had served. My mother told her the scrumptuous meal was hot dogs and beans.

The band Four Hits and A Miss consisted of Stan Rice (left) on sax & clarinet, Julie Balson on piano, Harry Korman on trumpet, Eugene (Yudel) Kitty on drums, and Isaac Korman on trumpet.

Simcha was kept busy in the store. When it was quiet in the store, he would play his favourite card games, poker and pinochle. He would also participate in the fund-raising events for the shul where these games were played.

My brothers and I were kept busy with school, cheder, Young Judaea, extra-curricular activities, and helping my father in the store after school. When my father went out to buy second-hand furniture for the store, he'd get us to come and keep the store open.

Our cheder teachers were Rabbi Katz and Mr. Sharony. We attended until we had our bar-mitzvahs. Rabbi Katz was the *shoichet* and I remember him coming to the house to *shecht* the chickens. My uncle, Michel Korman, used to give us our haircuts.

Willie Korman being carried by teammates on the Noranda Red Sox baseball team after their championship win, 1955.

I played in the Noranda High School band; we played at all the dances and also other venues. I played the trumpet, Yudel Kitty played drums, Stanley Rice played sax, and Chaskel Korman played trumpet. Murray Rice played the piano, but he was in a different band. Music was in the family; my father played the fiddle which he learned from his father, and my brother Willie had an ear for music. He picked up the sax and began playing almost immediately by ear. I played trumpet, and practiced every day after school.

Sonny was born in 1931. He wasn't into sports, but played a really good game of ping-pong.

Gordon Korman.

There used to be a little hill on the corner of Murdoch and 9th Street where the Noranda Recreation Centre (now called Dave Keon Arena) was built. That is where he honed his ping-pong skills. He worked for a number of years at Quemont Mines and moved to Montreal in 1957 after all of us had moved. He studied at night school, became an accountant, married Nancy Shuster and has two children, Cheryl and Lisa.

I was born in 1934 and moved to Montreal after high school

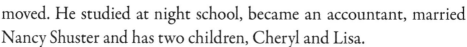

and started work in the shipping department of a company. Later, working in an accounting and bookkeeping role, I went to night school and became a CA. I moved with my wife, Bernice Silverman and son Gordon to Toronto in 1971. At fourteen years old, Gordon became Canada's youngest published bestselling children's author. Some forty years later, he is a no. 1 New York Times best-selling author specializing in middle grades. He just published his hundredth book, has four more in the pipeline, and is still going strong.

Willie was born in 1936. He was really into sports. He played hockey, baseball and rugby. He was the star pitcher on the champion Noranda baseball team. He moved to Montreal after high school in 1955, and took his B. Com at McGill and M. Com at Laval University. He received his Chartered Accountant designation from Laval. He later moved to Toronto.

Henry was born in 1938. He played baseball and hockey. He moved to Montreal after high school in 1956 and became a mechanical engineer. He married Regina Rubinovitch. They have two children, Shari and Jeffrey.

My mother moved to Montreal in 1956 when her youngest, Henry, moved. My father moved in 1957 after taking care of his business activities in Noranda. Our whole family lived together on Esplanade in Montreal. §

The Kravitz Family History
by Faygie Kravitz

M̲Y FATHER, SAM KRAVITZ (nicknamed Schmerel) arrived in Rouyn with his wife Rachel. He was the community milkman under the name Rouyn Dairy. Like Tevia in the movie *Fiddler on the Roof,* he delivered the milk with a horse and wagon.

My parents had three children: Goldie, followed one year later by Sally, then me, Faygie, ten years after Sally. Sadly, my mother of blessed memory, passed away when I was two and a half years old. My father remarried and my stepmother, Bella Spivak, raised me with the help of my sisters.

When I was thirteen, I moved to Montreal and lived with my sister Goldie, attending Monkland High School. I took the commercial course and upon graduation, I began working in the offices of an architect. I shared an apartment with Shirley Rice.

Milk delivery by truck, Rouyn, March 1965. (Societe d'histoire de Val d'Or).

While on vacation in the Catskills I met my husband, Martin Edelstein. He was from New York and I moved with him to the Big Apple. Tragically, Martin took sick and passed away. We were married for only seven years and this was a very difficult time for me. I remarried and my husband's name is David Baltch. He is a lawyer and is now retired. We have two children, Eric and Donna.

In New York, I worked as the office manager for an orthopaedic surgeon and retired when he closed his office.

My sister Goldie Schachter, of blessed memory, worked in

an office in Montreal. She married and raised three children. Her daughter Joyce is an obstetrician-gynecologist in Ottawa. Roslyn, of blessed memory worked in the office of a clinical director at the Jewish General Hospital in Montreal. Her son Stephen worked in several different fields.

My sister Sally Caplan, of blessed memory, married and raised two daughters. Gail Caplan Steinberg is an attorney in Montreal. Her sister Rhonda Struzer was a renowned chef in Toronto, and is now retired.

Milk delivery wagon, Rouyn, 1947. (Canadian Dairy and Ice Cream Journal)

Eventually my father, of blessed memory, moved to Montreal to be closer to his children and grandchildren. §

Esther & Max Martin appear at right in this photo, with Sam & Ethel Korman and Temel Korman on left.

Max and Esther (Shinehoft) Martin
by Honey Martin

ESTHER SHINEHOFT AND Max Martin were born in the same hospital on the same day on December 11, 1912 in Englehart, Ontario. They grew up in Timmins, went to the same schools, and on New Years Eve in the year of 1933 they were married. On September 27, 1934 their son Howard was born.

Max continued to work in his father's delicatessen in Timmins until it closed in 1940, then the family moved to Rouyn–Noranda. Their daughter Sandra was born on March 28, 1943.

Max worked in a hardware store until he took his salesman job in Sidney Sandberg's menswear store. After Sidney died in 1951, Max continued on as manager helping Esther Sandberg as much as possible for several years. Eventually about 1961 he purchased the business from her and changed the name to Martin's Menswear.

Max and Esther lived in the fourplex that Sidney Sandberg

built. The Shinehoft sisters, Rae Mednick, who stood at five feet, and Esther Martin, at five foot nine, walked together to Rouyn from Noranda to Kresges for tea every day but Wednesdays (when all the stores were closed). All throughout the town they were known as the long and short of it.

Both Howard and Sandra moved to Toronto when they were eighteen years old. In high school Howard was a star basketball player. Max Martin and his bridge partner, Max Garmaise, who were life masters, won the Noranda–Rouyn duplicate pairs tournament in 1952. Max Martin's family still have the trophy. The two Maxes used to bring bridge pairs to Rouyn, rent a room at the motel on Saturday nights when the store closed and played bridge until Sunday evening.

Max was highly respected and always involved in the community and the Kiwanis Club. In 1983, Max sold the store so he and Esther could move to Toronto to be with family. On that occasion the community hosted a Max and Esther Martin roast dinner and dance at the Hotel Albert as a sendoff. It was attended by dozens of people, and the departing couple was presented with a beautifully framed picture of Osisko Lake.

Both Max and Esther lived happily in Toronto into their nineties. §

Mirrel & Shlaime Mednick, circa 1918.

The Mednick family in their shtetl of David Horodek in the late 1920s.
Top row, from left: Sarah (Mednick) Isenberg, Shlaime Mednick, Sam
Mednick, Esther Mirrel (Korman) Mednick, Beryl Mednick. Front row,
from left: Libby Bregman (cousin), Dorothy (Mednick) Deuitch.

Growing Up Years
by Rosalie (Mednick) Nepom

A SENSE OF COMMUNITY and trust embraced me when I walked, freely and safely, from Noranda to Rouyn. I'd go into many of the stores where staff knew me and many were friends or colleagues of my parents. I could walk into the Ritter's store, choose a winter coat and without deposit take it home to show my mother. This came only from a sense of trust and friendship.

A sense of combined community with the non-Jews showed itself when the ladies from the synagogue would participate in a tag day for the charities of the area and sell apples for the local Cubs and Boy Scout troops. A sense of Jewish community working together pervaded our fund-raising efforts to build and keep up the synagogue and the Jewish school. The most popular fundraisers were the socials and poker games run by the women and held in the shul basement. The money raised by a percentage raked off from the pot of each game helped to keep the shul and its activities going for many years. Many of us children can remember the phone calls at 2 AM and later, demanding that the husbands come home. I remember my dad coming home at 8 AM following the poker game and after first opening his store.

Cheder: We attended the cheder or Hebrew school classes in the shul after school from Monday to Thursday. We learned about our history, culture, reading and writing in Jewish and then in Hebrew; depending on the teacher, we even got some conversational Hebrew. I remember five teachers — Rabbi Katz, Mr. Diamond, Mr. Goldstein, Mr. Sharony and Mr. Bloom, who also served as the community spiritual leader. After I moved to Toronto, Mr. Goldiner followed Mr. Bloom for one year and then Mr. Sharony returned and was the last community spiritual leader in Noranda. The cheder classes continued throughout the school year from September to June.

Young Judaea: Another use of the synagogue was our involvement in the Canadian Young Judaea Organization (*see page 213*). Young Judaea had programmes every Sunday morning in the synagogue's upstairs section. The rich programming included music, folk dancing, arts and crafts, and theatrical productions for the community's enjoyment. Each year a different town hosted a convention throughout the organization's northern region: besides Rouyn–Noranda in Quebec, the towns included Kirkland Lake, Timmins, Sudbury and North Bay in Ontario. It was a great way to meet many of the Jewish families throughout the northern district. Thanks in large part to Young Judaea, young people from Jewish families in Noranda and Rouyn kept very busy with Jewish activities, in addition to the sports and extracurricular activities involved in a regular school year.

Sam & Zelda in Paris en route to Canada.

How DID OUR FAMILY get to Rouyn–Noranda in the first place? For that, I need to delve a little bit into family history.

Sam had already been to Timmins, Canada and worked with his brother Yossel (Joe) Mednick for Mr. Frank Feldman. When they had enough money saved up, Sam returned to Horodok to bring his family back to Canada. Then his mother suggested that he marry someone from their hometown as opposed to a Canadian girl. She had heard that Zelda Farber was a very

10.
      <u>Miril, Berel and Dvora Mednik</u> - This is the case of a widow aged 49 years, her son aged 21, single, and her daughter, aged 15, single, all citizens and residents of Poland of Hebrew race. In July, 1930, Sarah Mednik, a resident of Haileybury, Ontario, and a daughter of the first named alien, submitted an application for the admission of her parents and the brother and sister referred to above, and as these people were then admissible under the relationship clauses of the regulations, the Department issued a letter to facilitate their entry. The father was, however, unable to pass medical inspection due to tuberculosis and the family did not come forward. The father is now deceased and the relatives in Canada wish the remainder of the family to join them. In addition to the daughter who originally submitted the application it is stated that there are two sons established in Noranda, Quebec, as merchants and that these relatives are in a position to receive and properly maintain the proposed immigrants. Representations in support of the application have been made by Mr. Jerry Abrams, of Englehart, Ontario, and by Mr. D. Koman, of Englehart.

This Order-in-Council of the Privy Council of Canada provided needed approval for Mirrel, Beryl and Dvora (Dorothy) Mednick to enter Canada as landed immigrants. Dated May 8, 1931. (LAC, OIC 1077, vol. 1483, p. 5.)

nice girl and suggested to Sam that he meet her. So he followed his mother's advice and six weeks later, on July 27, 1931, my father and my mother, Sam Mednick and Zelda Farber, were married. It was a small wedding ceremony because Sam's father, Shlaime Mednick, had recently died from tuberculosis. The wedding was held in a village near David Horodok, Russia, in the larger home of Zelda's aunt which could accommodate more people. Mom told me that for her wedding she wore a black dress which she remodelled from a dress that came in a parcel from America.

Shortly afterwards, the young couple left for Canada with Sam's mother Esther Mirrel, his sister Dorothy, and his brother Beryl. His sister Sarah came later and married an Isenberg (see page 54). Almost all of Zelda's family perished in the Holocaust.

Unfortunately the trip did not go smoothly. Mirrel, as she was called, was not well and the family was detained in Paris for several

September 9, 1947.

With reference to the proposed immigration of your relative now in Italy, we are in receipt of another advice from HIAS, Paris requesting us to attend to the matter of transportation funds.

We would like to repeat here that the transfer of relatives from Italy where there are no Canadian Immigration officials stationed, involves a great deal of formalities and expenditures, and it has been the practice of HIAS to accept a deposit of the prospective sum of these expenditures.

In this case we have been asked to secure from you the amount of $350.00 which is designed to include all transportation and other expenses from Italy through France to Canada. Upon the arrival of the immigrant HIAS will render detailed account of their outlay.

The interests of all concerned would require that you attend to the matter without delay. We shall be glad to hear from you as soon as convenient and remain,

Yours very truly,

Ernest M. Suessman
Consultant

EMS:DMG

23562

September 5, 1947.

Re: Chaim FARBER-It 104.945 Car

Mr. L. Neikrug, HIAS,
27 Rue de Berri,
Paris 8, France.

Dear Mr. Neikrug,

We are in receipt of your letter of August 30th dealing with the above named.

In the matter of having an immigrant file transferred to a country where there exist examination facilities, we would like to reiterate that we can approach the authorities in Ottawa with the request of that nature only when there is sound evidence that this migrant will be temporarily admitted to that country.

In the light of our experience we deem it extremely inadvisable to have a file rushed, say, to France, when the prospects of the migrant's admission to France are weak.

That would necessitate redirection of the file and disregarding the loss of goodwill in Ottawa, this procedure would also inevitably lead to painful delays.

May we suggest that you reread our previous correspondence on the subject.

As to the travelling expenses involved, we have complied with your request and approached the Canadian relatives on the subject; we will report further in due course.

Yours very truly,

Ernest M. Suessman
Consultant

EMS:DMG

Air Mail

Copy to Rome

These letters, involving HIAS, JIAS and the Immigration Branch of the Dept. of Mines and Resources, pertain to the emigration of Chaim Farber, Zelda Mednick's brother, from Europe to Canada in 1947. The Mednicks were instrumental in bringing Farber to Canada; he lived in Rouyn–Noranda for one year. More details, page 207. [CJArchives]

COPY
_____

DEPARTMENT OF MINES AND RESOURCES

Immigration Branch   File: B 20961

Ottava, Ont. March 26, 1947.

Dear Madam:

In connection with your application for the admission
to Canada of your brother, Chaim Farber, this is to advise that
the settlement arrangements have been found satisfactory and the
necessary steps are being taken for the examination of the proposed
immigrant overseas. It will, of course, take some little time to
complete these arrangements.

Yours very truly,

(sgd.) H.U.McCrum,
District Superintendent.

Mrs. Zelda Mednick,
109 Eight Street,
Noranda, Que.

Chaim Farber,
UNRRA Italian Mission
Transit Camp N. 1,
Bari,
Italy.

HIAS OF AMERICA
(HEBREW IMMIGRANT AID SOCIETY)

Central-Office for Italy – Sede centrale per l'Italia   ROMA, August 30, 1947
                                                              VIALE PARIOLI 10
Telegr.: ITALHIAS ROMA   Telef.: 873-965

                                                              open file?

To   : Jewish Immigrant Aid Society
            of Canada,
        M o n t r e a l,
        - - - - - - - - -

From : Hias – Rome,

Subject : FARBER Chaim – It 104.945 SABA

Gentlemen :

For your information please find attached a copy of a letter
from Department of Mines and Resources Immigration Branch, Ottawa, of
March 26, 47, addressed to Mrs Zelda Mednick, 109 Eight Street, NORANDA,Que.
sister of the a/n.

We would appreciate it very much, if you could approach the
authorities there, together with the sister of our emigrant and arrange that
the Canadian Consulate in Paris be authorized to issue the entry visa directly to the a/n person.   This suggestion was made by our Headquarters in Paris
in order to speed up the procedure of admission of our applicants in Italy,
without being obliged to wait for the arrival of the Canadian Commission.
This Commission is still travelling in Germany and Austria and we assume it
will take a considerably long time till they will come to Italy.

We have further been informed from our Headquarters Paris that
up to now no funds have been deposited in behalf of the a/n, and therefore,
we would suggest to contact the a/n sister of our emigrant in order to
induce her to provide the travelling costs, which amount to $ 350.

                                                      Sincerely yours,

Encl ; as stated.

By Airmail   for LEON D. FISHER
                                                      Director
cc/Hias – Paris   Hias – Italy

JM/mw

JEWISH IMMIGRANT AID SOCIETY
OF CANADA
RECEIVED
4)180
SEP 4 1947 A.M.
            P.M.
ANSWERED

Seated: Zelda Mednick (left), Rae Mednick, Norma Scott, Rebecca Ritter. Standing: Sam Mednick (left), Joe Mednick, Louis Scott, Jack Ritter. Noranda, circa 1950s.

months because of her heart condition. They were not allowed passage on the ship until she was better. We do not have any history whether Dad got a job to support them or if he had enough to last or if Joe sent money from Canada, but somehow they survived in Paris and finally were allowed to sail to Canada. My mother told me that she was sick throughout the trip and did not leave her room while the others went about and had a good time. Zelda also lost twenty-five pounds and came off the ship with a cane because she was so weak.

The family arrived at Pier 21 in Halifax as did many other immigrants coming from Europe. They travelled on until they arrived in the small twin mining towns of Rouyn–Noranda.

It was in the town of Noranda where Sam's Aunt Shaindel and Uncle Joe Korman lived. Shaindel was a sister to Sam's mother Mirrel and gave the young couple two rooms in their home to live in. Sam went to work in Joe Korman's grocery store.

Sam was friends with the postmaster of Noranda, Pete Firlotte. Mr. Firlotte was instrumental in arranging and guaranteeing for Sam a loan for $500 with the Royal Bank of Canada, thus enabling Sam to build a grocery store at 109 - 8th Street. The building included a three-bedroom home behind the store and five apartments above.

As for Sam's siblings, Sarah married Albert Isenberg, Joe married Rae Shinehoft, and Beryl went to a yeshiva in Brooklyn, New York, and became a rabbi. He was the first yeshiva-graduated rabbi in Quebec City and served from 1937 to 1944. Dorothy lived in Rouyn–Noranda until her mother died in 1941 and then she lived with the Isenberg family in Rouyn for a while before marrying Danny Deuitch and moving to Montreal. Their stories are told elsewhere in the book. My grandmother, Mirrel, is buried in the Palmerston section of the Dawes Road Cemetery in Scarborough.

Sam and Zelda Mednick raised a family of three children (Sol, Rosalie and Eddie) in Rouyn–Noranda.

Sol moved to Toronto and was involved in remote hunting and fishing and camping properties. He married Marni Shore and has three children, Beth, Jason and Marshall.

Rosalie became a registered nurse, and has a daughter, Evelyn.

Eddie graduated as an opthalmologist and is married to Robin Henry. They have four children, Samuelle, Milton, Mordy and Zale. §

Sam Mednick stands in the doorway of Sam Mednick Grocery, Meat and Beer.

Memories of a Grocer's Son
by Sol Mednick

MY FATHER SAM MEDNICK and his bride Zelda Farber left for Canada shortly after their wedding in 1931 with Sam's mother, Esther Mirrel, his brother Beryl, and sister, Dorothy. Sam had previously settled in Timmins, worked and saved money to journey back home to David Horodok, Poland to bring the family. After a harrowing trip and delays in Paris, they arrived and settled in Rouyn–Noranda.

My father opened up a store, called Sam Mednick Grocery, Meat and Beer at 109 - 8th Street. On the weekends and sometimes after school, it was my responsibility to keep the store in order. I would clean and restock the shelves, make sure the labels of the items were aligned properly facing outward, and generally tidy up the premises, including the basement inventory storage areas. My father always dressed professionally in a shirt and tie and was kind

The arrow indicates the location of Sam Mednick's Grocery Store at 109 – 8th Street. The building was declared a municipal heritage site in 2018.

and accommodating to his customers. On Sundays when the store was closed, he would take care of the bookkeeping and accounts receivable as the store's customers bought their groceries on credit. If they had money, they would shop at the A&P or Dominion stores. Many of the customers were immigrants from Eastern Europe and spoke Polish, Russian, Italian and Ukrainian. As my father also spoke these languages (except Italian), his customer base continually expanded as more immigrants arrived. They appreciated his knowledge and willingness to speak their languages. Although my father didn't speak French, his employees did, so French customers were also able to shop using their own language. Some clients would put groceries in their pockets to avoid payment; we were aware who they were and would position ourselves where we could watch to see what they took. After they left, we would add those items into their charge accounts.

The beer sales and customers were always exciting. I recall we sometimes had visits from Mr. Molson of Molson's Brewery; as part of managing his business he would regularly visit all his vendors. When he was in the store, if someone came in to buy beer, we would steer them towards buying the Molson brand. This would please him a great deal and he would invariably pay for the customer's case of beer. The bootleggers, who all were situated within 1000 feet of the police station, were very good clients of the store. Their businesses flourished particularly on Sundays, Wednesday afternoons, and evenings when the store was closed. They mostly sold beer to miners and others who lived in the boarding houses. I would go with our driver, Lucien Manseau, every Monday morning to pick up the empty beer bottles from the bootleggers and return them to the beer supplier. There was a 50-cent profit for each empty case of pints and 35 cents for each empty case of quarts.

Our suppliers were all local. They included Gamble and Robinson's Wholesale Grocers in Noranda and Lafortune and Gagne in Rouyn. Fruit and vegetables were from Quebec Fruit.

These companies would send their trucks to the Toronto Food Terminal regularly and bring back the supplies to Rouyn–Noranda. We bought our meat from local dealers such as Schneider's, Fried and Teitelbaum.

My father was also in the blueberry business and bought basket loads of berries from the pickers who brought them to our grocery store. The berries grew in various localities outside of town, such as around Lake Dufault and Donalda Mines. Sometimes the blueberry pickers would unscrupulously add an old shoe to make their 11-quart baskets appear fuller than they actually were.

We would use a strong fan during packaging to blow out the leaves and small branches from the blueberries before transferring them into other baskets for shipment.

My father would send them in refrigerated CNR rail cars to Mr. Fogel in Windsor or Detroit. Once each railway car was loaded for shipment, the door would be sealed with a special serial number as protection against theft.

My childhood friends, Stanley Rice and Howard Martin would sometimes drop by the store on a Sunday afternoon when my father was doing his accounts and I was restocking the shelves. Stanley loved olives and would take a bottle of olives from the shelf, open it, and gobble down a few. If he were around to read this memory, I'm sure it would put a smile on his face.

The store was quite large — about 2500 square feet. At the back of the store was a door that led into our relatively spacious three-bedroom home. It was very convenient to live in the same building, as our "commute" took less than a minute. My parents, sister Rosalie, brother Eddie and I always had dinner and supper together as a family. I also remember that, after my sister, Rosalie was diagnosed with polio at age three, my mother had a wringer washing machine in her bedroom to wash the compresses used to treat her polio. We used to have to take long drives to Montreal on a gravel road for her appointments with the specialist, Dr. Goldbloom.

Wilfred Malouf, a driver with the Mednick grocery store, sits in his truck, circa 1950.

Downstairs from the store and our home was the basement which was used to store inventory. It was also the location where our butcher prepared the home-made sausages using the sausage machine. He used meat and cutovers of scrap meat — nothing went to waste. Our customers loved them. For our family meat consumption, my father ordered kosher meat from Swift Canadian in Montreal. When Rabbi Katz came over to *shecht* the chickens, he occasionally came across a chicken he deemed as *traif* (non-kosher). In that case, the chicken was sold to the Royal Young Hotel and Grill, who had their restaurant across the street. Charlie Young was one of the store's clients. As I said, nothing went to waste.

Upstairs from the store there were five apartments. I remember when I was about ten years old, a horse and buggy with groceries from a competitor, Superior Grocery, pulled up to deliver groceries to a tenant. I couldn't understand why the tenants would buy groceries from someone else when they lived in such proximity to our store. At the time, I was watering the large garden in our backyard. Without thinking about what could go wrong, I aimed the hose directly at the horse's "private parts." Needless to say, the horse reared and bolted down the laneway; the wagon full of groceries overturned. Acting very nonchalant, I pulled the hose into the building, shut the door, and quietly went upstairs. A while later, I ventured outside to see the result. There were groceries everywhere — what a mess!

Later on, my father built a two-storey home at 14 – 6th Street. We lived on the main floor and there were two apartments upstairs. These apartments were rented out and the rent paid our mortgage.

During the 1950s, Nordy Nosov, originally from Iroquois Falls (Ansonville), would drive to Noranda to visit with cousins and friends. One particular evening around 10 p.m., we decided to drive to Val d'Or, Quebec, about sixty-seven miles away, to visit family members and friends. But our group, which consisted of Nordy, me, Howard Martin, Stan Rice, Murray Rice and Isaac Korman, faced a significant problem: we needed some gasoline for the car and all of the service stations were closed.

Fortunately, Howard had siphoning equipment in his basement that was kept for this particular purpose. Even though it was after hours, we quickly realized we could obtain gas from the trucks of Dallaire Dairies, which had evidently been used for this purpose once before. Murray Rice evidently had some previous experience in the siphoning of gas. But when he began to suck on the hose to draw the gas from the tank, some gasoline lodged in his mouth and throat, leaving him with an awful burning taste.

The only way to resolve the burning sensation was to go to my dad's store to get some Wrigley's chewing gum.

While we were there, we noticed a police car driving towards us. The constable, Leo Leblanc, wanted to know why we were at the store at this very late hour. I tried to explain that I was checking the furnace to make sure there was enough coal in the furnace.

Leblanc had a strong feeling we were up to no good, and suggested we go home and call it a night.

We never got to Val d'Or.

The Rescue of A Lost Immigrant

MR. NICK LITWINKO from Ukraine had already been in Canada for seven years and was living in Rouyn–Noranda. In 1930, his wife, Vera (Andrekevich) Litwinko left her home in Terebiezov to join him. Before leaving, her favourite brother taught her to sign her name and drove her in his horse and cart as far as Poland. On November 30 she reached Liverpool and boarded HMS Adriatic to sail to Canada. In Halifax she was held in immigration detention because she didn't have enough money. When the money finally arrived she was able to board a train to Montreal, and then to Rouyn–Noranda.

It would have been difficult enough for a thirty-three-year-old woman with no money, who had never travelled on ships and trains, and who couldn't speak the language. But the worst was yet to come. When she got off the train, her husband was not there. Not knowing what to do, she finally broke down in tears. Inadvertently, she had gotten off the train at the wrong station.

To her luck, a kind gentleman approached her and was able to communicate in Ukrainian. He figured out that her husband would be waiting for her at one of the other three train stations in the area. That kind stranger was my father, Sam Mednick. He was able to persuade Mrs. Litwinko that he could take her to her husband and that's exactly what he did.

Vera Litwinko never forgot what my father did for her that day, nor did her daughters.

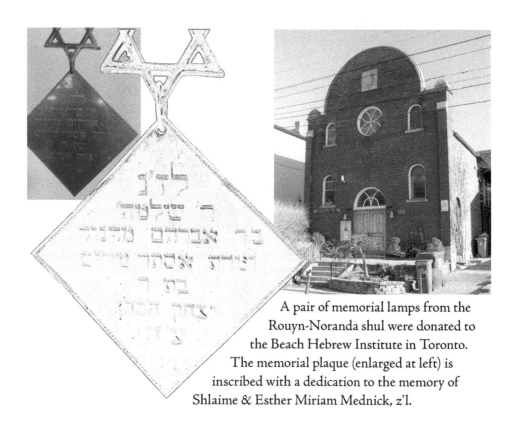

A pair of memorial lamps from the Rouyn-Noranda shul were donated to the Beach Hebrew Institute in Toronto. The memorial plaque (enlarged at left) is inscribed with a dedication to the memory of Shlaime & Esther Miriam Mednick, z'l.

Rouyn–Noranda Memorial Lamps

Inside the Noranda shul, to the right of the Ark, were two memorial light fixtures. They had been donated to the shul when it was first built by the children of Mirrel and Shloime Mednick: Sam, Joe, Sarah Isenberg, and Rabbi Beryl. When the shul was sold in 1972, I acquired the lamps on behalf of our families. Wishing to find a way to honour our grandparents, I approached the executive of the Toronto Beach Hebrew Institute which agreed to install the memorial fixtures in their synagogue.

The lamps were refurbished, polished, and rewired before installation. Attached to the lamps were memorial plaques that read: "Dedicated to the memory of Mr. Shlomo [Shlaime], son of Avraham Mednick and Mrs. Esther Miriam, daughter of Mr. Yitzchak the Cohen." §

From Russia to Rouyn-Noranda
by Ed Mednick

I WAS THE LUCKIEST KID in the world to have had the parents I had.

My dad, Sam Mednick, came over in 1927 for the first time. According to the passenger manifest, he had only five dollars to his name at the time. But soon he had earned enough money to go back to Russia to bring his parents and family over. While back in Russia, he got married to my mother, who was one of the most beautiful women in their town. They fell in love and got married within six weeks.

My mother, Zelda Farber, had been engaged to a man from their village in Russia who had gone to Palestine. She had papers to follow him there but, after she met my father, she gave the papers to her sister, Chaika. She went to Palestine and ended up marrying the man who had been my mother's fiance. My mother chose my Dad instead because, as she later told my sister Rosalie, she felt he was a very good man and that life would be better in Canada than in Palestine.

My father brought over his brother Beryl as well as his mother and sisters, Dorothy and later Sarah. His siblings always looked up to him and over the years he and my mother helped them all. My parents

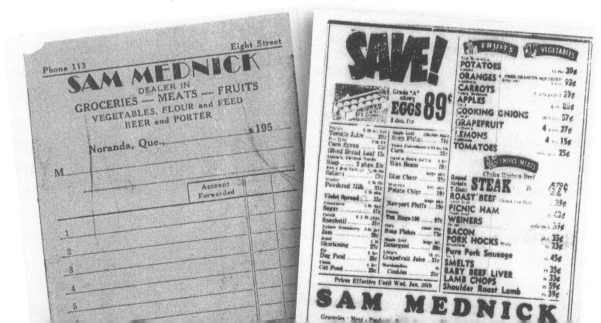

also sent bags of food and clothes to help Chaika and her family in Palestine.

Sam Mednick was a respected business and family man, known for his kindness and his intelligence. He treated his grocery customers with respect. When they could not pay he helped them with discounts and told them they could pay later. Among the roughly forty Jewish families in Noranda, he was always held in the highest esteem. He would arrange for huge barrels of pickles and black bread to be in shul for the end of the Yom Kippur fast so that everyone could have something to eat on the way home.

Sam's parents were Shlaime and Mirrel Mednick. Sam's mother had been a Korman and was a sister to Shaindel who married Joe Korman. In the Jewish world, it was common for cousins to marry in those days. My parents moved in with Shaindel and Joe for a few years upon coming to Canada. My father then opened his own grocery store. My mother, who was very smart and well-respected, took care of the house and made sure we were all fed, clothed and healthy. She was also involved with my father's business decisions, for example insisting on building two apartments over our house for rental income.

For these reasons and many more, I regard myself as being blessed to have the parents I had. §

Joseph & Rachel (Shinehoft) Mednick
by Stanley Mednick

ISRAEL JOSEPH (JOE) MEDNICK was born in 1902 in David Gorodek, Pinsk, Russia (now Belarus). His mother was Esther Mirrel (Korman) Mednick; his siblings were Sam Mednick, Sarah Isenberg, Beryl Mednick and Dorothy Deuitch.

In 1921 Joe came to Canada and went to Englehart, Ontario. Later he went to Timmins. In November 1926 he became a naturalized citizen of Canada.

He was introduced to Rachel (Rae) Shinehoft by Golda Horwitz. Rae was born in 1907 in Englehart, Ontario. She lived in Tomstown Township, Ontario and later moved to Timmins. Her siblings were Esther Martin, Manny Shinehoft and Max Shinehoft.

Joe and Rae were married in Timmins on September 2, 1928 by Rabbi Wolf Linder. They moved to Noranda where Joe worked with his brother Sam in the grocery business. He left the grocery business and opened up a combined menswear and ladieswear store on 8th Street. In the back of the store was their home. In 1941 the store burnt down and Joe

relocated the menswear business to Main Street in Rouyn.

Joe bought a two-bedroom house at 180 First Avenue (now Fredric Hebert) in Noranda and the couple made a Jewish home at that location. They moved there with two of their children, Dolores born in 1930 and Hinda born in 1935 in the Youville hospital. Their third child, Stanley, was born in Youville in 1944.

In 1950 Joe closed the menswear shop in Rouyn. The following year he opened a mining machinery business using the garage in the backyard as the warehouse to store the inventory. About a year later he purchased land and five buildings in the McWatters neighbourhood and relocated the business there. In 1957 it was renamed Mednick Metal Company Limited.

On July 30, 1950, Dolores Mednick married Maury Bloch. This was the first wedding held in the new synagogue on 9th Street in Noranda. The close-knit Jewish community shared in preparing the food for the reception. They have three children as well as grandchildren and great-grandchildren.

In 1955 Hinda married Joe Brody in Detroit, Michigan. They have three children as well as grandchildren and great children.

In 1969 Stanley married Barbara Weisdorf in Toronto. They have two children as well as grandchildren.

While in Noranda, Rae's favourite activity was her daily walk to Rouyn with her sister, Esther Martin, for tea at Kresges. In 1970

Stan Mednick

Mednick Metal Company Limited was sold and Joe and Rae moved to Toronto. That same year Rae passed away.

In 1971 Joe married Yetta Miller in Montreal, officiated by Rabbi Beryl Mednick. They set up a Jewish home in Toronto and were together until Joe passed away in 1984. The family remained a close unit until Yetta passed away in 2011. §

Miller family, from left: Sarah Miller, Debbie Miller, Bernadine Miller, Marvin Miller, Ben Miller.

Rouyn–Noranda Experiences
by Bernadine (Miller) Harrar

MY FAMILY WAS probably the last Jewish family to arrive in Noranda. I was born in Trail, British Columbia and my brother Marvin and sister Debbie were born in Kelowna. We moved to Noranda when I was eight years old. My grandmother, Goldie Miller, insisted that my father Ben move back to Noranda to help manage Miller's Store.

As kids, we were very busy with cheder, Young Judaea, music lessons, Lake Dufault in the summer, hockey and skating in the winter. We were never bored.

The shul was an important part of our lives, and not just for the learning from our teacher, Mr. Sharony. If you arrived before he did, you could get the key from the Rice's, who lived across the street.

View of Main Street, Rouyn, showing Kresge's and Miller's, a women's and children's clothing shop, circa early 1960s. Miller's originally belonged to Goldie and I. J. Miller. It was then owned by Harry Miller and Ben Miller, with a small portion by Rose (Miller) Korman.

You could go downstairs and play ball hockey until class began. We kept a bunch of hockey sticks and balls hidden in the furnace room. Boots were used as goal posts. Joe and Marvin were usually the first to arrive and play ball hockey and also usually the last to arrive after Mr. Sharony would sound his cowbell ding-a-ling to summon us.

Slicha in Hebrew means excuse me. We all used this word at least once during cheder class to go to the bathroom. From there, we stayed in the social hall and played hockey until the teacher noticed that too many students were missing.

Mr. Sharony once got so frustrated with our lack of discipline that he slammed the door to the cabinet so hard that he broke the glass. He turned to Debbie, the quietest one of the bunch and motioned to her to clean up the glass with the broom. Poor Mr. Sharony had a lot to deal with. It is truly amazing that he stayed despite our bad behaviour.

At Young Judaea, my group was led by Mona Garmaise for

many years, and she taught us Hebrew songs and dances. We learned a lot of Israeli dances and became quite good at that. The local TV station decided to start a cultural exchange and invited a few dance groups to perform. We were the first ones and we were so excited! On the appointed day and time, as we were ready to start, the technician asked Mona if it was really necessary for us to hear the music. He was having some technical difficulty and didn't understand that we had to hear the music in order to dance to it. Fortunately, the problem was solved and we were a big hit.

Young Judaea gave us many years of fun experiences. In the dead of winter, we had an inter-city *kinus* or weekend gathering. We went to a different town in the north every winter and were billeted in each other's homes. We travelled by the Ontario Northland Railway (ONR). It was always dark and there was usually a snowstorm. We were curious, fidgety adolescents. On one such trip, we left our train wagon and were exploring the rest of the wagons. After about a half hour, we noticed that things had gotten very quiet. We looked outside, and indeed, we were on a deserted train track and the rest of the train was taking off. Luckily, we were able to run along the train and jump back on!

We all had music lessons. Some of us learned piano, my brother Marvin and cousin Joe Miller learned guitar, and Harvey Korman was really cool and learned saxophone. Harvey belonged to a band, so Esther and Kathy and I would go to encourage the band. (Kathy and Harvey are siblings and we are all cousins.) It helped that they practiced in the social hall of the shul. We actually made lifelong friendships with some of the guys in this band.

In about 2010, the opportunity arose for me to show my oldest son, Miki, and his fiancee, Lianne, where we lived. We flew to Noranda and walked around for hours visiting the places that were so dear to me. The whole city of Noranda had just bought these big green garbage bins. It was the law that each house or establishment had to

have the same bins outside for garbage. We walked through the lane of the shul that is now a little apartment building. That building had three garbage bins and someone had taken the time to paint the letters in clear, Hebrew lettering, BEIT KNESSET. There were no Jews in Noranda in those years, but someone, who knew the history of that little building, had taken the time to figure out how to paint the Hebrew letters. Awesome!

OUR GRANDPARENTS WERE I.J. and Goldie Miller. I didn't have much of a chance to know I.J., my grandfather, as he passed away a few months after we moved to Noranda. Goldie was a business woman and the brains behind Miller's Store. She spoke nine languages and insisted that we all learn French. She said that she couldn't speak French and she needed it. In her later years, she sat in the store beside the cash, and received her friends and customers. They were all Eastern European ladies and she spoke to them in their native languages.

Other important elders in our lives were Michel and Temel Korman. I think that Michel Korman was the unspoken leader of the Jewish community. He was the president of our little shul for a long time and placed the cornerstone which is still visible on the front of the building. Temel was a nurturing, stay-at-home Bubbie. She cooked in huge quantities, and her home always smelled delicious. Even after they moved to Montreal and were living in an apartment with a galley kitchen, she continued to receive and nurture whoever passed by. Brenda, Jack Weinstein's wife, tells warm, wonderful stories of the times spent with them in Montreal. Jack and Brenda inherited Temel and Michel's dining room set and have it to this day.

Group at Lake Dufault, July 20, 1960.
❧ Front row, left to right: Marvin Miller, Esther Korman holding Jeff Wise, Debbie Miller, Maury Weinstein.
❧ Back row, left to right: Joe Miller, Jerry Korman, Laurie Miller, Harvey Korman, Jack Weinstein, Kathy Korman.

Our parents and grandparents all contributed and assured the upkeep of the shul, and ultimately our Jewish education. They brought in a number of teachers to teach us to read and write Hebrew. It must have been tough on the teachers as many of us were not particularly interested or attentive. The boys all had nice bar mitzvahs.

Once a teacher in cheder broke a yardstick over Harvey's head. The broken pieces remained on the blackboard ledge for many years. To our grandparents' and parents' credit, almost all of us married Jewish mates and carried on many Jewish traditions.

The Storm

As MENTIONED, WE spent a lot of our summer days at the Miller cottage on Lake Dufault. In our young teenage years, a parent would drive us to Dufault, leave us there for the afternoon, and come to get us after work.

When I was about thirteen years old, my cousins and I decided to hike out to Dufault. We alerted our parents and reassured them that we would not walk along the highway, but we would take a shortcut

At the Miller cottage at Lake Dufault, Marvin Miller, Debbie Miller, Esther Korman and Bernadine Miller enjoy a boat excursion.

through the slag. The slag is what the mine throws away after they have melted the rock and removed all the valuable minerals. It is a red, metal residue that was systematically thrown over acres and acres of bush land, creating a vast metallic moonscape upon which absolutely no vegetation can grow.

My cousin Laurie Miller, who is very smart and one year older than me, suggested that we follow the train tracks, cross a train trestle and gradually make our way to Dufault. The train trestle was a high bridge over which the railway tracks extended across the slag. There is no place to walk except on the rails and railway ties. We agreed to check for a train before attempting to cross. We were a little group. Laurie Miller and Jerry Korman were the oldest. Then there was me. Esther Korman is Jerry's sister. The youngest ones were Marvin, my brother and Joe, Laurie's brother.

It was very overcast, but we decided to go anyway. We took bathing suits and a few towels. I don't think anyone took a raincoat. Water bottles and sunscreen hadn't been invented yet.

As luck would have it, it started to rain exactly as we were crossing the trestle. It was a really heavy storm with a lot of thunder and lightning. Marvin and Joe were ahead of us, so they were the most advanced on the trestle.

The wind was out in all its fury. The storm was so bad that we couldn't hear each other. Somehow, Laurie got us to turn around and get off the trestle. Now just to put it into perspective, Laurie, Jerry and I were heavy enough to be able to hold ourselves on that trestle. Esther was small and thin, but Marvin and Joe were just children, real lightweights. They were almost at the other end. Somehow, they understood that we were returning. They had the good sense to crouch down and crawl back so as not to be blown away.

We all made it off the trestle but our misery wasn't over. The lightning was pretty close and there was a danger of being hit. Laurie seemed to think that the railroad tracks would attract the lightning, so we found a little lean-to, beside the tracks. Laurie found some wooden shingles and insisted that we stand on them for protection from the lightning.

Marvin and Joe were really wet and cold, so we wrapped them in whatever we had that was sort of dry. Esther insisted that she was okay although her teeth were chattering. So we waited in the lean-to, on the shingles, for the storm to abate, and eventually resumed our journey to Dufault.

Later that evening, we found out that we had been caught in the tail end of a tornado. It likely hit us while we were on the trestle. Luckily we are Northerners and pretty hardy. Lucky for us that G-d or our angels were watching over us! §

View of Lake Osisko with Noranda Mines across the water.

Adventures and Misadventures
by Marvin Miller

WHEN I WAS THIRTEEN, all of my uncles from Winnipeg and Los Angeles came to Noranda for my bar mitzvah. We invited all of them out to Dufault one Sunday afternoon. We decided to do some water skiing. I had been watching our next door neighbour who was an expert water skier come speeding into the dock and intentionally spraying everyone who was watching, and I wanted to do the same. But as I came speeding in, I slipped and hit my head really hard. Still, I got up out of the water with a big smile, as I wasn't going to let anyone know that my head was killing me. I pretended that nothing was wrong and it had all gone the way I had planned.

Ice skaters on Lake Osisko, with Youville Hospital at left.

PHOTO J.H.BOLDUC

When I was about fourteen or fifteen, I got some friends together and proposed that we go to Dufault for an overnighter. Somehow I got my hands on some high-proof alcohol. My cousin Joe Miller and I and several friends set out for Dufault together. I don't remember how we got there.

This was in the middle of winter and I remember wandering around erratically on the ice. I also remember that we brought some TV dinners to eat and that my friends had vandalized my dinner and thought it was funny. The experience taught me that alcohol was not for me.

Dufault was a really important part of our childhood experience together. When we were younger, usually Bubbie (Goldie Miller) would drive me and Joe to the chalet and stay with us and feed us. As we got older, my uncle, Isaac Korman, would let us use his 40-horsepower Johnson and we saved up our allowances and sold pop bottles to get gas for the boat. I remember very well schlepping that big gas can all the way down to the corner gas station and then trudging back to the chalet with the full gas tank.

Our one responsibility was to cover the boat with the tarp to protect it against the rain. One time we neglected to put the tarp on, and it poured and the boat got swamped. Uncle Isaac was really upset with us, but to our surprise he got over it and still let us use the boat after that which we were very grateful for because we couldn't live without water-skiing.

Just before I headed to McGill in 1967, I got a job working in the smelter of Noranda Mines. At first I worked on the copper furnace, removing the blocks that stopped the hot copper after it was poured. Then I was asked to go into the furnaces and, using a jackhammer, drill out the bricks so that they could be replaced. They only gave me salt tablets and a paper mask as protection.

I also worked along the railroad tracks inside the mine for a while. These jobs enabled me to save money for McGill University. §

Few Jews Left In My Father's Hometown

by Mira Miller (Reprinted from heyalma.com, 2021)

MOST PEOPLE associate Jewish communities in North America with big cities, so it's no surprise when someone asks where my father is from and my response elicits a confused or bewildered reaction. No, he's not originally from Montreal (the city I grew up in), I tell them — my father was actually born and raised in Rouyn–Noranda, a small French mining town in the Abitibi-Témiscamingue region of Québec, Canada.

My parents and I made the eight-hour drive to my dad's hometown in the summer of 2017, heading 600 km northwest of our house in the suburbs of Montreal into the heart of mining country. My father had been talking about showing my mother and me where he grew up for as long as I could remember, but I was far more eager to visit Los Angeles — where he spent most of his twenties — than a tiny, unknown town that required a day-long car trip. Little did I

know that what I would see, learn and experience during that trip would change and define my identity as a Jewish person.

While it's true that the majority of Jewish communities across the continent reside in big cities, there was once a time when Jews purposely relocated to small mining towns in search of business opportunities in the *shmatta* (garment) industry, as well as in other sectors and professions.

My great-grandparents were no exception. They founded Miller's, a department store located on the town's main street that was beloved by the community for decades. My grandparents, Norma and Harry Miller, moved from Montreal to Rouyn−Noranda in the mid-1940s to help out. The Jewish community, consisting of roughly forty families at its peak, lived largely harmoniously with the town's residents for many years.

My father, Joseph Miller, was born the youngest of three children in 1950. He lived in Rouyn−Noranda for the first sixteen years of his life before departing for university, just as most other Jewish kids from the town did as soon as they were old enough to leave.

When he returned with his wife and daughter in tow roughly fifty years later, much of what he remembered of the town had changed. It was clear almost immediately upon arrival that it had become primarily francophone and homogenous in the years since he

had left for the big city — with just ten Jews living in the town of 42,334 residents as of 2016.

This was technically unsurprising since most anglophone communities, including Jews, departed Québec's small towns for other parts of Canada in the 1970s due to language politics and the rise of the province's separatist movement. But it didn't make it any easier to accept that the community in which my father had come of age — the community from which I came, too — had completely vanished.

Walking down the main drag, we received confused looks as we conversed unapologetically in English. It was clearly not something the locals were accustomed to hearing. But while there were hardly any Jews left living in the place my dad had once called home, we did find the facade of the synagogue — where he once attended Hebrew school four times a week and had his bar mitzvah decades ago — untouched.

The three of us stood in shock and awe as we stared at the plaque that read *Kneseth Israel Congregation*. The interior of the building had been converted into apartments, but the Hebrew writing and Magen David remained on the exterior brick wall as proof that the community existed.

This shul was once far more than an old building where the religious prayed, I soon learned — it was the central gathering place of the Jewish community. Similarly to how places of worship serve as community hubs for small, immigrant communities in towns and cities across North America, this synagogue was where happy occasions were celebrated and tragedies were mourned.

"Being there in shul, seeing the Torah carried around, it gave me a sense of identity, of who I was," my father, who considers himself a secular Jew, told me of what the synagogue meant to him as a child.

In the basement, a large multi-purpose room frequently doubled as a place for my dad and his cousin to goof off before Hebrew school. The two boys played endless hockey games in that room using just a rubber foot from a chair and broomsticks, according to my father. And a stage in that same space saw countless theater productions rehearsed and performed, some of which were directed by my grandmother. Her love of theater, something I fortunately inherited, forever keeps me close to her despite her death in 2010.

Before I visited Rouyn−Noranda at age twenty, the small town in northwestern Québec with a thriving Jewish community was, for me, simply a hypothetical setting in which my dad's childhood anecdotes took place. I felt hardly any personal connection to this town that was so far from my own upbringing, and so different from what I knew of today's modern Jewish communities. It was sometimes difficult to believe it even existed in the first place.

But standing there, smack in the middle of this town, I could picture my dad's stories of community, laughter, and love taking place right before my eyes.

"It was very affirming for me to come back to say we were here, we existed, we lived," he told me as we recently reminisced about our trip.

Driving by the four quaint homes in which my father was raised and many family members came to stay, I could feel the tight-knit Jewish community that found a way to thrive in a town in which they were both a religious and a linguistic minority. And I could feel that a huge part of my Jewish identity today was rooted in that place, whether I was aware of it or not.

This is a common story for many Jews. As a people that has been consistently displaced throughout history, it can be difficult to truly understand where we come from, especially when our ancestors' communities seem so far off from our own realities.

Whether it be the shtetls of Eastern Europe that vanished in World War Two, the Jews that were forced to flee violence in Ethiopia in the 1990s, or any other Jewish community that dwindled into nothing over the years, many Jews will never have the luxury of visiting the places where their parents, grandparents, and great-grandparents made homes for themselves, or see the actual structures where their stories unfolded. And yet we carry the remnants of these communities with us, often unknowingly, in our day-to-day lives.

I was fortunate enough to actually see the physical place where my dad, now seventy, was raised, and I will be forever grateful for how it opened my eyes to the importance of these now-vanished communities, and to our duty to keep the memories of them alive.

This town, which could arguably be considered one of the least Jewish places in present-day Canada, helped me feel closer to my Jewish roots than I ever thought possible. Because while it is no longer inhabited by Jews, the architectural evidence of the community's existence and my father's accompanying memories helped show me where I come from — and there is nothing more Jewish than learning about, and honouring, the people and places that came before. §

Miller family photo from mid-1950s. Front row, from left: Norma Miller, great-grandmother Esther Weiner, grandmother Goldie Miller. Back row: Harry Miller, Laurie Miller, Judy Miller, Joe Miller.

The Miller Family of Rouyn–Noranda
by Judy Miller

I WAS BORN in Montreal in 1943 and when I was two years old, my parents, Harry and Norma Miller, moved us to Rouyn, Quebec. My paternal grandfather Isaac John Miller ("I. J.") was born in Minsk. He emigrated to Montreal via Halifax when he was nine years old. At the age of eleven, he started a cap manufacturing business in Montreal. He met my grandmother, Goldie Weiner, in 1911 in Montreal where she was working in a garment factory on Papineau Street.

Goldie was born in Austria in 1893. Her father worked for Emperor Franz Josef as a groomsman in charge of the Lipizzaner horses. He was killed while trying to get the horses to safety during the First World War. Her widowed mother, my great-grandmother, Esther Weiner, brought her children to Montreal.

I. J. and Goldie were married in Lachine on July 1, 1911. They settled in Outremont after having moved to Winnipeg and Fort Frances, Ontario, seeking business opportunities. They had six children, Ben, Tillie, Harry, Morris, Rose and Arlene. They moved to Rouyn–Noranda in 1936 and opened the family clothing business called Miller's Store.

My dad, Harry, who was born in Fort Francis, met my mother Norma Loeb, who was from Winnipeg, in Trail, British Columbia, where they were both working. They married there and moved to Montreal.

My father worked as a draughtsman for Harrington Tool and Die Company and my mom was a nurse. In 1945 my grandmother asked my dad to move his family to Rouyn–Noranda as she needed his help in running the business.

We rented a duplex on Mercier Street in Rouyn, next door to Sam Kravitz, who owned the building.

In 1946 my brother Laurie was born, followed by Joe (Joey) in 1950. I went to grade one in the English Protestant School in Rouyn along with Faigie Kravitz and Ruthie Fried; the Frieds were our neighbours across the street.

During that period there was a great fire that wiped out most of Main Street in Rouyn including Miller's Store. My father was awakened by a call in the middle of the night informing him that the store was on fire. He rushed out into the night, ran into the burning building and managed to grab the safe that contained the store's ledger showing all the accounts receivables. Since most of the store's business was done on credit, those records were vital and thanks to my dad's heroism, the business was saved and they were able to reopen in a new location.

At first they set up headquarters in the basement of the Albert's

A major fire on March 17, 1949, wiped out numerous businesses on Rouyn's Main Street, including many owned by members of the Jewish community. (See also the story "A Shopkeeper's Diary," page 171.)

Hotel. The townspeople who had been patrons of the store and had outstanding charge accounts, understood the dire situation the Millers were in and came to pay what they owed, to help them get back on their feet. My grandmother spoke several Slavic languages, which endeared her to the large immigrant population (we called them DPs or displaced persons then) who settled there to find work in the mine. In addition, the fact that people were able to shop at Miller's Store on credit and pay off their account when and as they could, engendered their loyalty and earned their trust. My grandmother was an amazing business woman who devoted her life to her entrepreneurship. My father was equally loved and respected by customers and staff.

In 1949 my dad opened a shoe store in Malartic and we spent

a year there, during which Joey was born. We returned the following year to Noranda and moved to 5th Street to an apartment building owned by Dr. Ironstone. Our neighbours across the hall were Fanny and Eddie Weinstein.

My dad and mom continued to work in Miller's Store until he once again branched out on his own and opened the Pfaff Sewing Store on Main Street in Rouyn where he sold Pfaff sewing machines and Elna knitting machines. I was tasked at eight or nine years old with sitting in the window demonstrating the sewing machine. The demonstration included doing rows of multi-coloured embroidery, sewing on a button, making a buttonhole and sewing a wooden ruler to a piece of cloth. People were most impressed that the machine was so strong and so simple to use it could be operated by a child. Inside the store my mother demonstrated the knitting machine, which could knit a whole row at a time and make a dress in a day. I still have her Pfaff sewing machine which still runs like a charm seventy years later.

Ultimately my dad and mom returned to Miller's Store where they worked until my grandmother Goldie passed away in 1963. My mom was the creative genius who designed the store windows that had the town talking about her originality — which included having live models in the windows. The models would hold a pose until someone stopped to look at the window. Then they would change their positions, to the shock of the viewers, who would then burst into laughter.

I attended Carmichael and McNiven elementary schools in Noranda and then Noranda High School where I graduated in 1960. My brothers followed suit. After living on 5th Street we moved to B Avenue in Noranda and then we moved to a new house my dad had built in the New Townsite.

Arlene left Rouyn–Noranda in 1953 and married Ted Wise from the Trail–Rossland district of British Columbia. They were married in the Kneseth Israel Synagogue in Rouyn–Noranda in 1953. I was

Goldie & I.J. Miller

ten years old and a very proud maid of honour. The next wedding to take place there was my own on June 10, 1962.

Arlene and Ted settled in Montreal where Ted practiced as a pharmacist. They have one son, Jeffrey and two grandsons, Gregory and Lucas. In partnership with Morris Goodman of Montreal, Ted went on to found Pharmascience, one of the largest pharmaceutical manufacturing companies in Canada.

Rose remained in Rouyn–Noranda where she married Isaac Korman and had two children, Jerry and Esther.

Several years after we arrived, Ben moved to Rouyn–Noranda with his wife, Sarah, and children Bernadine, Marvin and Debbie, and joined his siblings, Rose and Harry, in the family business.

Morris left Rouyn–Noranda after high school and entered McGill University where he studied medicine. He specialized in gastroenterology and became Chief of Gastroenterology at the Jewish General Hospital in Montreal until he left to practice medicine in Houston, Texas. He married Montrealer Lucy Heilig and they had two children, Vicky and Jonathan.

Tillie married Montrealer Harry Cohen and they had two children, Bobby and Ellen Sue. Bobby married Montrealer Cindy Bercuson and they currently live in Atlanta, Georgia. Sue married Usher Barnoff of Montreal and they moved to Calgary where they currently reside.

After the death of my grandmother Goldie, my father sold his share of the business to his brother Ben and he and my mother moved to North Bay, Ontario, where he bought a ladies dress shop which he renamed Miller Modes. The business attracted many new customers and my parents thrived there.

Sadly their enjoyment of their new home was to be cut short by my father's untimely death in his early fifties. My mother continued to run the business on her own for a couple more years but it was becoming too much of a burden for her. Since neither of my brothers was interested in running the store it was sold and my mother relocated to Montreal where she resumed her work as an X-ray technician. After she retired she spent several winters in Israel on a JNF-sponsored work/travel tour. She planted trees, volunteered in Hadassah Hospital and tutored soldiers in English. Her dream of visiting Israel with my dad was never realized as he died before it could take place. She passed away in 2009.

I left Rouyn–Noranda for Montreal at sixteen after completing high school. My plans to attend university got postponed after I met my future husband, Harold Perlman. I worked in the accounting office of Zellers and then for Bryan Engineering before becoming engaged at age eighteen and returning to Rouyn–Noranda to await my upcoming wedding.

The wedding was a community affair with everyone from the community invited. Montreal guests who had never been further north than Ste. Agathe came for a weekend of fun and festivities. They all stayed at the Motel Henri where the reception took place, including my Uncle Morris, Aunt Lucy and their regal black standard poodle, Pietro. The kosher chickens were sent in from Toronto. The wedding was officiated by a "kosher" rabbi, Rabbi Lehman, who was brought in for the occasion, and assisted by Mr. Sharony. The very able and entertaining emcee, Mr. Justice Max Garmaise, was able to keep the crowd distracted until the much delayed meal (someone had forgotten to turn the ovens on) was served. The event rated a full write up on the social page of the Rouyn–Noranda Press.

After spending a summer in Fredericton, New Brunswick, my new husband and I moved back to Montreal and settled in to domestic life. I gave birth to my daughter Janice on April 22, 1965 and my son Monte on December 21, 1967. Suffice to say I didn't get to see much of

Expo '67 that year.

In my thirties I returned to school and studied communications at Concordia University. I went on to have a thirty-year career in the non-profit sector as a fundraiser and public relations professional. I worked for several organizations in the Jewish community including Jewish National Fund, the Saidye Bronfman Centre and Mount Sinai Hospital. I ended my career with a nine-year stint as director of development at the Montreal Oral School for the Deaf — a most rewarding and fulfilling experience, made all the more meaningful by the fact that my father had had a profound hearing loss most of his life. Upon retiring at age sixty-nine, not feeling ready to be a retiree, I returned to school to obtain a certification as a personal fitness trainer, which I continue to work at currently. My clients, including my Aunt Arlene, are all seniors who are committed to remaining fit and able for as long as possible.

I returned once to Rouyn–Noranda for the Noranda High School fifty year reunion. Although it was fun to revisit my childhood home, I found I had left that part of my life behind many years before and the place held little nostalgia for me. My fondest memories are of our rustic little cottage on Lake Dufault where half the Jewish community used to converge on any given weekend. Sleepovers there with my friend Faigie Kravitz were the best. Memories of the meals my mother cooked on that old wood burning stove still make my mouth water. My parents cooked the pike and pickerel my father had just caught over an outdoor fire on the beach. We had so much freedom as kids then, that would be unthinkable today. My mother made sure we all had music lessons, and I also had dance training and gymnastics which I still use today in my third career as a personal fitness trainer.

Because my mother was a nurse she got a job for two summers at Camp Hagshama and took us three kids along in lieu of salary. It was there I discovered the unbelievable joy of living in a world where everyone was Jewish. The experience was profound and made me the

Noranda High School Reunion, August 1990 (outside the former synagogue).

&❧ Front row, seated (left to right): Murray Rice, Stan Rice, Sol Mednick, Tanya (Garmaise) Feldman, David Garmaise, Isaac Korman.

&❧ Middle row, seated (left to right): Norman Ironstone, Hinda (Mednick) Brody, Rosalie (Mednick) Nepom, Carol Rice, Faye (Sandberg) Goldfarb, Mona (Garmaise) Klein, Bernadine (Miller) Harrar, Reggie Korman, Doreen Korman, Sid Ritter, Jacqueline/Jody Isenberg, Hartley Isenberg.

&❧ Standing (left to right): unknown, Pearl (Fried) Deuitch, unknown, Marilyn Ironstone, Shirley (Rice) Kalfin, Chaskel Korman, Henry Korman, Marsha (Sandberg) Feldman, Rose Korman, Jerry Korman, Esther (Korman) Verred, Nancy Korman, Sonny Korman, Bernice Korman, Ami Verred, Rae Rice, Eddie Rice, Ruth (Ritter) Miller, Meyer Isenberg, Al Deuitch.

ardent lifelong Zionist I am today. It made me aware of how much I missed living and growing up in a Jewish milieu. I remember on a visit to Montreal, being on a streetcar and being dumbfounded to see someone sitting nearby wearing a Magen David and reading a Yiddish newspaper. Unimaginable to me! §

Solomon Pekilis, I.J. Miller, Arlene Miller, Goldie Miller, unknown, Rouyn–Noranda, July 1941

The Pekilis Family
by Stanley Pekilis (as told to Isaac Katz)

MY FATHER, SHLOMO (Solomon) arrived in Canada from the Ukraine in 1918. He was thirteen years old and arrived by himself. He was raised by his two uncles who had clothing stores in two towns north of Quebec City. His uncle Nisel Ortenberg was in Saint-Casimir and his uncle Itzik was in La Tuque. He eventually made his way to Montreal where he met and married my mother Bayla (Betty) Spector in 1928.

My older brother Morris was born in Montreal and the family moved to Quebec City where my father worked as a salesperson in a clothing store. I was born in Quebec City in 1934. Later, in 1936, my father went to La Sarre, Quebec to work in another clothing store. The depression was causing much difficulty for people, and they had to do what they did to earn a living. While my father was in La Sarre, my mother, brother and I moved back to Montreal.

Then in 1940, my father moved to Rouyn to work for Mr. Miller who had a store on Main Street. We joined my father soon after and lived on Perrault Street. We moved to Noranda in 1943. Eventually, my father opened a clothing store on Main Street.

I graduated from Noranda High School in 1952 and the family moved back to Montreal. I obtained my degree in Accounting from McGill University and my Bachelor of Commerce from Loyola while I was working in the field of finance. In 1971, we moved to Toronto where I was employed by the government of Canada and eventually went on to work for the Ontario government. I was able to graduate from York University with a Master of Business Administration.

My wife Betty and I have two daughters, Susan and Ellen. Ellen has blessed us with our granddaughter, Lilly, who is currently attending university. §

	No. 1	No. 2.
		Surname first
Name of Groom	*[This Ontario record shows the marriage of Isaac Rice, 25-year-old farmer, & Rosa Goldford (Goldfarb), age 18. The couple were married in New Liskeard, Nippissing district, Ontario, on January 18, 1906. They arrived as pioneers in Noranda in 1925.]*	Rice Isaac ✓
Age		25
Date of Marriage		Tp. Chamberlain Jan. 18, /06
Place of Marriage		New Liskeard
Residence when Married		Tp. Chamberlain
Place of Birth		Presky Russia
Bachelor or Widower		B.
Occupation		Farmer 013944
Name of Father		Israel Rice
Maiden Name of Mother		Hannah Goldford
Religious Denomination		Jew.
Name of Bride		Goldford Rosa
Age		18
Residence when Married		Tp. Chamberlain
Place of Birth		Pinky, Russia
Spinster or Widow		S
Occupation		,
Name of Father		Samuel Goldford
Maiden Name of Mother		Yhitta Goldsmith
Religious Denomination		Jew
Names and Residences of Witnesses		Samuel Solomon New Liskeard Jessie McLachlin New Liskeard
By Whom Married		Rev. F. E. Pitts
License or Banns		L.
Date of Registration		Jan. 18, 1906
REMARKS	25	

Isaac Rice opened this general store in Noranda after his arrival in 1925 during the town's pioneering days. The building later became a hotel.

The Rice Family, Jewish Pioneers of Rouyn–Noranda
by Shirley (Rice) Kalfin

M Y FATHER EDDIE RICE and grandfather, Isaac Rice, were pioneers of Rouyn–Noranda. They arrived in 1925 when my father was only eighteen years old. My grandparents had emigrated from Russia in their early teens; my grandmother (Rose Goldfarb) at fourteen and grandfather at sixteen. They had made their way to Canada unmarried and were married in New Liskeard, Ontario in 1906. On my mother's side, her father, Itzik Korman, had spent seven years separated from his family working on the Ontario Northland Railway to earn enough money for their passage to Canada.

My earliest memories are of a small tightly-knit family that lived close by and were involved in our lives by proximity, and love. Neighbours on both sides were not Jewish but the synagogue was directly across the street from our house, and both sides of that building were occupied by Jewish families. The Ritters, the Ironstones, Isaac and Rose Korman, Olga and Frank Cohen, the Steinberg family, and the Luke family all lived across the street from us. Then down the lane were the Millers, and Uncle Michel and Auntie Temel Korman. Next block was Nachman and Sonia Korman, Norma and Louis Scott, the Sandbergs and the Martins. I could go on to name all the members of the congregation but I think you can see that the whole community was within a stone's throw from our house and all were very much a part of our life since most of them were related to us in one way or another.

The languages we heard while growing up included Yiddish, Russian, Polish and French. We learned to speak and write Yiddish so that we could communicate with our grandparents and we learned to speak French as a normal course of events.

My mother and father, Rachael and Eddie Rice, were both schooled in Canada. My father was born in New Liskeard and my mother came from Russia at an early age; she went to Central Tech in Toronto and studied music at the Royal Conservatory there. My parents were unusual in the community since the parents of many of my contemporaries were immigrants who struggled with English.

The synagogue was very much a focal point of our Jewish community. We all went to cheder after school and participated in the youth activities sponsored by Young Judaea which included conventions in Kirkland Lake, Timmins, Sudbury and North Bay. At that time there was no television and most movies were forbidden by law to children under the age of sixteen. We needed a gathering place and the synagogue served that purpose.

Weddings and bar mitzvahs involved everyone in the community and often included members of the entire northern Jewish community

E.O'Reilly
C.E.Stock
G.A.Clark
M.S.Rudd
F.Riley

W.R.Welk
B.BAril
S.RIce
J.Smith
A.W.Quesnel
L.Beauchamp
E.Rice

Club HockeyRouandas
dans les années 1930

Sam and Eddie Rice, both sons of Isaac and Rose Rice, were players in the local team, Club Hockey Rouandas, as shown in this 1930 photograph.

as they were, of course, either related or "landsmen" who had come from the same village or town in Europe.

At that time in our town, there was no such thing as a catered affair. The food preparation was done by members of the community and each household contributed their specialty. Toby Ironstone made the best cole slaw and Mrs. Fried made the best cabbage rolls and, of course, we had to have Rose Korman's pareve chocolate cake. My own grandmother's specialties were bagels and strudel.

I realize now that most members of our community were staunchly Zionist and they made an effort to instill that same fervour in the younger generation. There were visitors and speakers who came from the big city to bring us up to date on events in Israel. We

Delayed registration of birth for Eddie Rice, son of Isaac & Rose Rice of Rouyn, Quebec, born in Krugerdorf, Ontario in 1907. Registered in 1928.

were encouraged to go to Camp Shalom and Camp Biluim and some of us went on to spend a year in Israel. Hadassah was an organization that was important to our mothers and they spent many hours raising money with rummage sales and card parties.

Outside our little community, however the atmosphere was not always so welcoming and loving, and we were exposed to anti-semitism as an everyday part of life. The children next door taunted us with calls of *"maudit Juif,"* there were ugly stares in the compulsory Scripture class when we studied the New Testament, and places like the Golf Club didn't accept Jews. These were realities that we were taught we must be prepared to face. When I left home to go to "the city" and subsequently look for a job, I knew that I must make sure that possible employers were aware that I was Jewish before accepting any position.

A funny thing that I remember in all of that discrimination was the incongruity that my mother was invited to be a member of the Imperial Order of the Daughters of the Empire (a bastion of white anglo-saxon ladies). She did join and played an active role in that organization.

I recall my great aunt, Esther A. J. Korman of Val d'Or,

attending the burial of her mother in Toronto and after the service she and her sisters-in-law were visiting all the family graves including that of Auntie Esther's husband, A.J. Korman. When one of her sisters-in-law said, "Esther, why don't you say something to A.J.!" Auntie Esther walked up to his grave and in Yiddish said "A.J., get yourself up, we're going to have a cup of coffee!"

Laughter and tears came easily to all of us. The imminent death of a favourite cousin brought the congregation together to perform a "renaming" service in the hope that the angel of death would make a mistake and take someone else in his place. They knew it was to no avail but needed to hope.

I once said to a group of young women in a religion class at Queens that the reason that I remained Jewish was partly because the world around me would never let me be anything else. As time goes on I realize that it's bred in the bones. I am a proud Jewess with a heritage that goes back centuries.

I can't close without saying that our upbringing gave my brothers and me a great respect for our elders who had the ability to laugh at their problems, and who needed no intermediaries to communicate with Gd. They spoke directly to him, bearing their souls and complaining about their lot. At the same time it seemed to be understood that whatever it was would have to be dealt with, and they just did. They were the ultimate realists. §

One of the last of the old-time Jewish residents of Rouyn–Noranda, Eddie Rice is shown outside the former synagogue with Mme Casse–Gauthier.

Reminiscences of Eddie Rice

From the journal, Continuité (1989)

Eddie Rice, son of a Rouyn–Noranda pioneer, was part of one the first Jewish families to settle in the city. In 1989 Annette La Casse-Gauthier, president of the Abitibi-Témiscamingue Heritage Society, collected his memories for the benefit of the readers of the journal Continuité. The article appeared in issue no. 45.

MY FAMILY CAME from Russia to settle in Toronto. In the years 1910–1911, my father worked for the transcontinental railroad and he lived in Cochrane, Ontario. He had three businesses along the railroad: one in Cochrane, another in Porquis Junction and the last in Iroquois Falls. They all burned down in the great forest fires of 1916.

The family returned to Toronto and then, a few years later,

moved north to Englehart. When Rouyn opened, my father came to work there. The smelter of the mine was not yet built; it was in 1925. I arrived with the family in 1926. The work was hard and my father, who was very ambitious, worked very hard, like all the immigrants who had come here to improve their situation.

Noranda did not yet exist. My father opened a general store near Rouyn. Eventually we were forty-five Jewish families and every month, each one gave money for the construction of the synagogue, according to his means.

The first synagogue was contructed of wood; we rebuilt a new brick synagogue on the same site in 1949. Mr. [Michel] Korman was the president. The facade is in brick and the rest in stucco. Above the door is the inscription: KNESETH ISRAEL. To the right, at the bottom of the building, is the cornerstone. It bears the name of M. Korman, our president, and the year of construction.

The basement was set up for social gatherings and the first floor was reserved for worship, with a classroom for children. At the top there was a balcony for women to pray.

The rabbi, Mr. Katz, lived around here and the students went to the synagogue every day. The children grew up and left for university and then left Rouyn–Noranda. The community began to dwindle; they could no longer finance or maintain the synagogue. Today (1989) we are only two families. The Lions Club bought the synagogue and sold it ten years ago. It has become an apartment building.

Occasionally we go to Toronto, Montreal or Sudbury for our meetings. Our three children have gone away. I've thought about moving sometimes, but, you know, after living here for sixty years. . . . §

FORM E.

PROVINCE OF QUEBEC—PROVINCIAL HEALTH SERVICE

STATISTICAL RETURN OF MARRIAGE

1. PLACE OF MARRIAGE—
County of _Noranda Que._ (Provincial county)   Civil Municipality of _____ (Write name and state whether city, town, village or rural municipality)

BRIDEGROOM	BRIDE
2. Full name _Jack Ritter_	12. Full name _Rebecca Erlichman_
3. Occupation _Clerk_	13. Occupation _Clerk_
4. Bachelor, Widower or Divorced _Bachelor_	14. Spinster, Widow or Divorced _Spinster_
5. Age _25 Twenty five_	15. Age _23 Twenty-two_
6. Religious denomination _Jewish_	16. Religious denomination _Jewish_
7. Residence _Rouyn Que._ (Usual place of abode)	17. Residence _Rouyn Que._ (Usual place of abode)
8. Place of birth _Barza Poland_ (Province or Country)	18. Place of birth _Roumania_ (Province or Country)
9. Place of birth of father _Poland_ (Province or Country)	19. Place of birth of father _Roumania_ (Province or Country)
10. Can bridegroom read? _Yes_	20. Can bride read? _Yes_
11. Can bridegroom write? _Yes_	21. Can bride write? _Yes_

22. Date of marriage _Nov. 27_ (month) (day) 19_33_ (year)   23. By license or banns _Licence_

24. PLACE OF REGISTRATION OF THIS MARRIAGE—
(a) Name of Parish or Church _Jewish Congregation_   (b) Civil Municipality of _Noranda, Rouyn Que._

(c) Date _____ (month) (day) 19___ (year)   (d) County (Provincial) _____

25. Name of clergyman in charge of Registers of Civil Status in which

registration of this marriage was made _Rev. M. W. Katz_

Any person other than a clergyman registering this marriage will sign here _Rev. M. W. Katz_

(VOIR L'AUTRE CÔTÉ POUR LE FRANÇAIS)

109059

Quebec Statistical Return of Marriage
for Jack Ritter & Rebecca Erlichman, Rouyn–Noranda, 1933.

Memories of Rouyn–Noranda
by Sid Ritter

M<small>Y FATHER</small>, Mordechai Ya'akov Rytermann, came to Canada in September of 1929 from Bereza Kartuska, a town half way between Moscow and Warsaw (now located in Belarus) and made his way to North Bay where he had an uncle who was married and had six children.

With his limited knowledge of English he made his way to Timmins. He had heard there was a Jewish man, Sam Bucovetsky, who was hiring newcomers to work in his store. He was hired and worked as a stock clerk while he learned more English.

He was then sent to Kapuskasing to work in a new store which the company had opened. That's where he first met my mother, Rifka Erlichman, who was there visiting some friends from her home town in Khotyn, Bessarabia (Ukraine). She had come to Canada a few years prior and was living in Winnipeg because that is where her brother Joe Erlichman was living.

My father had four sisters. Fayga Bayla had come to Cuba a few years prior and then settled in New York.

Jack & Becky Ritter and their children, Sidney & Ruth.

Tova Chana and her husband, Tzemach Kosofsky, and two children all perished in the Holocaust. Shmuel Aziel, a brother, had died as a young child, as did Doba, another sister. Rifka (Rita) married Voveh (William) Weinstein: my father brought them to Noranda after the war; ultimately they moved to Montreal and had two children, Solly and Howard who now live in New York. My father's younger brother, Avrom Leib, perished in World War Two.

My parents, by then known as Becky and Jack Ritter, were the

Sidney Ritter, fishing.

Ruth Ritter with schoolbooks,
outside the synagogue.

second couple to be married in the original synagogue in Noranda. (The first couple was Walter Crotin and Sorel Korman (Temel and Simcha's sister) from Ansonville on March 19, 1933.) They were married on November 27, 1933. Rabbi Katz officiated at the ceremony and his signature appears on the ketubah. My sister Ruth, of blessed memory, was born in 1934 and I was born in 1936.

My father had a clothing store on Perreault Street in Rouyn. This store was unique because my father installed flourescent lighting which made the store very bright, allowing the customers to see clearly what they were purchasing. Local merchants visited my father to view this new technology, which quickly was adopted to brighten up other store interiors.

Ruth graduated from Noranda High School in June 1951. She was an avid basketball player and enjoyed her time on the school girls team. Our house was next door to the synagogue and Ruth would bake cookies to treat the kids going to cheder after school. She clearly was interested in nutrition and was aware of kids needing a snack if they were to learn. She went on to study nursing at the Jewish General Hospital and was part of the second graduating class in 1955. Ruth

Marriage of Hinda Craft & Sid Ritter, June 1958.
Left to right: John & Sadie Craft, Hinda & Sid, Rebecca (Becky) & Jack Ritter.

married Eli Miller, of blessed memory, in 1957, and they raised four children: Cindy, Frances, Toba and Merle. They were blessed with ten grandchildren. Later on Ruth returned to nursing until she retired.

I graduated from Noranda High School in June 1953. I then spent one year in Israel. Upon my return, I attended McGill University in the faculty of engineering. Upon completion of my first year, I transferred to the University of Manitoba in Winnipeg where I completed my degree in engineering. I went into the photography business. My specialty was in audio-visual technology and I was very gratified to participate in structuring the programs for schools and businesses.

I married my wife Hinda, of blessed memory, in Ottawa in June 1958. We then went to Winnipeg where we remained, raising four children, Michael, Beth Caren, Alan and Andrea. We were blessed with eight grandchildren. My parents, of blessed memory, joined us in Winnipeg in 1961. §

Jack & Becky Ritter with
son Sid, and Sol Mednick.

Sidney & Esther Sandberg, with Faye (left) and Marsha, Rouyn–Noranda circa 1950.

Rouyn–Noranda Memories & Genealogy
by Faye (Sandberg) Goldfarb

SIDNEY SANDBERG, MY FATHER, was born in Horodok, Pinsk Gubernia, now in Belarus, in 1902, and emigrated to Canada in 1923. He went to Toronto where he stayed with his aunt, Soreh Korman, his mother's sister.

My grandfather, David Korman's parents, Soreh and Shlaime Korman, had numerous children, sons Michel, Nachman, David, Joe, Esser, Sam, Harry (Hershel), Aaron and Itzik and one daughter Esther (AJ). Many of them moved to places in northeast Ontario and northwest Quebec.

Michel and Temel Korman, as well as Temel's brother Simcha Korman and his wife Dvoshe, moved to Noranda. Michel had a menswear store, and Simcha had a second-hand furniture store on Perrault Street in Rouyn. Michel's brother Nachman and his wife Sonia also moved to Noranda and opened a menswear store.

Esser and Bella Korman moved to Timmins and opened a dairy. It was called Korman's Dairy.

Itzik and Sonia Korman moved to Kirkland Lake and operated

a menswear store.

David and Chane-Fagel Korman moved to Englehart, opened a department store and a movie theatre. They had four children: Golda, Sam, Esther (who married Sidney Sandberg) and Nick.

Joe and Shaindel Korman moved to Noranda and opened a grocery store. Shaindel and Chane-Fagel were sisters. (Two brothers married two sisters). The sisters had another sister, Sorel, who married Beryl Bregman and lived in Sault Ste Marie. The Bregmans had four children, Dorothy, Isaac, Libby and Zelda.

Harry (Hershel) and Dasha Korman lived for a short while in Englehart before moving to Toronto. Aaron and Mary Korman lived in New York, and Sam passed away in 1928 at the age of twenty-four in a car accident.

Sidney Sandberg also migrated to northern Ontario. We believe he worked at the Noranda Mines. He built a fourplex at the corner of 6th Street and First Avenue, which was kitty-corner to the Noranda Hotel, and built a duplex next door on First Avenue.

Sidney opened a menswear store in Noranda, on 3rd Avenue and Eighth Street next to the firehall. He catered to a very ethnic clientele as he spoke many languages including Russian, Czechoslovakian and Ukrainian. The store catered to more of the working-man, many of whom worked in the mine.

He was known as a very loving human being and extremely trustworthy. Often his clients would give him their paycheques for safekeeping so they wouldn't spend it drinking over the weekend, as there was not much to do in the small towns. They would go back to Sidney on Monday to retrieve their paycheques in order to pay bills. Sidney was a master bridge player, an avid sports enthusiast and a great family man.

He married Esther, daughter of David and Chane-Fagel Korman, in Englehart on August 6, 1933. Sidney and Esther had Faye (me) in 1936 and Marsha in 1939.

Sidney later moved the store from Noranda to Rouyn's Main Street. Max Martin was the manager of the store until Sidney passed away in January 1951. Max and his wife Esther (nee Shinehoft) lived in the fourplex that Sidney built. Max continued as manager, helping my mother Esther for many years. Eventually he purchased the business from her and re-opened it as Martin's Menswear.

The store was located next to the Capital Theatre which was owned by the David Korman family (Esther's parents) and managed by Esther's brother, Sam Korman.

Sam Korman married Ethel Abel (from Port Elgin) in Noranda in 1946. They had three children, Kathy, Harvey and Sydney. Sam not only managed the Capital Theatre in Rouyn but also the Paramount Theatre. He also managed the Noranda Theatre. Sam and Ethel also lived in the duplex that Sidney Sandberg built.

Max Martin and his wife Esther (Shinehoft) had two children, Howard in 1934, and Sandra in 1946. Esther (Shinehoft) Martin's sister Rae married Joe Mednick and lived in Noranda. Esther and Rae's brother, Max and Rose (Nathanson) had a son, Sheridan, and lived in Timmins. Howard Martin and Sheridan Shinehoft were born a month apart and were best friends for life. Interestingly, Sidney and Esther Sandberg's daughter, Faye, married Max and Rose Shinehoft's son, Sheridan.

The northern Jewish community grew in part due to the large Korman family and their migration to northern Ontario and northwestern Quebec. §

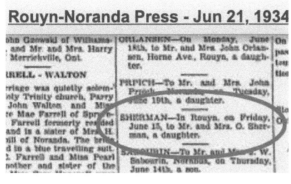

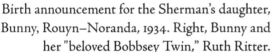

Rouyn-Noranda Press - Jun 21, 1934

Birth announcement for the Sherman's daughter, Bunny, Rouyn–Noranda, 1934. Right, Bunny and her "beloved Bobbsey Twin," Ruth Ritter.

My Rouyn–Noranda Years
by Bunny (Sherman) Shapiro

I WAS BORN ON JUNE 15, 1934 at Youville Hospital, one day before Sol Mednick.

My three sisters, Lamie, Susan and Debbie were all born in Noranda but, of the three, only Lamie was old enough to have some memories of our hometown.

My family left Noranda at the end of June in 1949 after the fire which started at Stedmans, next door to our store, and made its devastating way all along Main Street. We watched it from our home across the lake in disbelief. My father returned later that year and rebuilt the store.

Life had centred around elementary and then high school and after-school cheder at the shul. I still have fond memories of our cheder teacher, Mr. Sharony, because I still sing the songs he taught! I remember that some of us stood outside the classroom more than inside ....

Much after-school time was spent at the Ritter's home with my beloved Bobbsey Twin, Ruthie. Mrs. Ritter's cookies were delicious!

A sad memory was the discovery of Teddy, Sid and Ruthie's dog, lifeless on the street as we returned from school — a victim of hit-and-run!

And a vivid memory on the dark side: those poker games which were held at different homes. I remember the thick cigarette smoke, and the pile of money raised "as a rake-off" for the shul. The wives finally put a stop to that — at least to poker in their homes.

And . . . the smell of Noranda Mines! My father developed an asthmatic cough which he attributed to the fumes from the smoke stacks that frequently swept through town. One day, for the first time, he ordered coconut cream pie at the local Chinese restaurant. Somehow that pie relieved the congestion. And he continued to do so as long as he kept the store. Magic!

Much of my free time was spent at our store in Rouyn, where I "manned" the cash register and made a list of women who ordered nylon stockings. This was wartime!

And there was Young Judaea where somehow I became a club leader. That was the beginning of my love affair with Young Judaea that has lasted a lifetime.

We had a very small, but cohesive *chevrah* (circle). We saw one another not only at school and cheder, but socially as well.

I was very proud of the fact that Rouyn–Noranda had done its job in preparing me for entering grade eleven in a Toronto high school. §

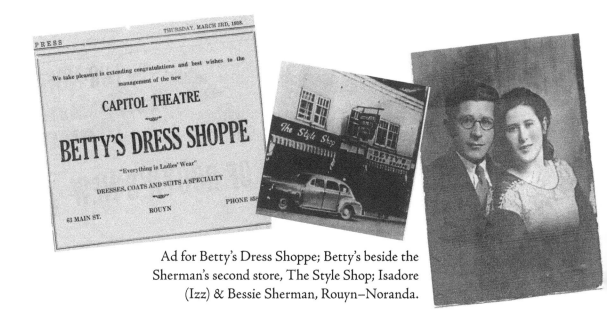

Ad for Betty's Dress Shoppe; Betty's beside the Sherman's second store, The Style Shop; Isadore (Izz) & Bessie Sherman, Rouyn–Noranda.

A Shopkeeper's Diary
By Bessie Sherman (as told to Ayala Shapiro Burg)

In the mid-1970s Bessie Sherman's granddaughter Ayala spoke with her about her and husband Izzy Sherman's long experiences as shopkeepers in Rouyn–Noranda. The couple ran Betty's Dress Shoppe as well as The Style Shop. Edited excerpts of the original conversation appear below.

ISADORE (IZZ) AND I WENT around for a couple of weeks to every wholesale manufacturer on Spadina (Toronto) to purchase dresses. We started our business with only $247 and we did not have a cent left to our name otherwise. On March 17, 1931, with a trunk full of dresses, Izz went up north. Rouyn–Noranda, Quebec was our destiny. Izz rented a room and advertised that he had come with new spring women's fashions. I stayed behind to go around to the wholesalers to buy new dresses and new things that were available. Everyday we would communicate by letter and I would replace the dresses he sold. I could spend only as much as he had sold each day.

In June, I left for Rouyn–Noranda. We rented a small store and living quarters on Perreault Street. We would work until 10 or 11 pm every evening and always were available if customers wanted to come after closing time or on Sundays. We would have been able to build up our business sooner if we had a way to finance the business. My Auntie allowed us to draw a hundred dollars on her account, and we knew this was our limit. And so, life went on. We did our best and earned very little and did not have enough merchandise to sell, but we were content.

Wartime and the Holocaust

IN 1939 THE WAR came and quotas came out and were based on what you were getting before. If we had bought ten dresses before, we were allowed only three or four now. We were stuck for merchandise. To compensate, Izz went off to Montreal to buy a different type of merchandise — towels, washcloths, sheets, pillowcases — items that were hard to get in Rouyn–Noranda. Izz bought bales of fabric by the yard to make bedspreads, and had them cut and seamed to sell. With this plan, we had merchandise to sell, when most stores were lacking stock. But after six years, we still did not have the finances and had to count each dress that was sold in order to buy a new dress to sell.

During the war years, back in Rouyn–Noranda in 1942, we all knew that our people were being massacred in great numbers in Europe. I cried day and night, thinking what was happening to all of them, including my mother, brother and all our dear ones.

The Store

ONE SUMMER when I was visiting Auntie in Toronto, Izz called to say that he had a chance to move to Main Street in Rouyn. We both knew that we were not solid enough in case we needed something extra, but I left it up to Izz to make the decision. When I returned in August with Bunny (our first child), I saw our nice little store on Main Street. In the back, out of the wood shack that was there, we made a kitchen, a bedroom, and a little living room for us. Gyp-rocked and papered, it looked very nice while the summer sun was shining, but when winter set in, we had ice under our beds and frost on the walls. The remarkable thing was that Bunny never once had a cold at that time. Later we moved upstairs above the store.

In 1941 our rental building came up for sale. A man came over to us and gave us the first chance to buy it. By some unforeseen providence we decided to buy the building which allowed us to have two stores. We expanded into children's wear and we built a basement to sell all sorts of household necessities. We were getting along very well except it was very hard work. We worked until 11 pm most evenings.

Bessie Sherman and Zelda Mednick.

The stores were open late twice a week plus Saturdays so there was not much time for recreation. But our Jewish community had lots of gatherings. We would attend when we could. I belonged to Hadassah. We made rummage sales and played cards. Interesting speakers and travellers (who sold wholesale items to storekeepers) arrived regularly and our home was always open to them. The travellers would come for coffee and sometimes for dinner and we are still friendly with some of them today. They also used to come for Christmas Day and work with us and other shopkeepers, continue their itinerary to the other northern towns and then return for a New Year's turkey dinner at our home. The speakers came to our community to collect money for Israel as the need grew after the Israeli Declaration of Independence on May 14, 1948. Our hearts were with Israel and we used to give very graciously.

So, our life in Rouyn–Noranda was a very busy one.

The Fire

EIGHT YEARS after we bought the building, fate stepped in and made a *pshurreh* (a story, as we say in Yiddish). A huge fire broke out and burned down our two stores and several other buildings. Our basement had just recently been finished. The painter had just finished his work in the basement the night before the fire and the new merchandise was moved in. It was March 17, 1949, St. Patrick's Day, and people were celebrating at the Stedman's store next door to us which was where the fire broke out. At 2 am, we were called to come out and we saw it all going down. So many years of hard labour and we had very little insurance on the building and merchandise. When we arrived, the roof was still on our store, but we could not get in to save anything because the firefighters said it was too dangerous to go inside as the roof was about to collapse. We had about a thousand dollars of deposits that customers had given us for new spring clothes. Later we advertised that these customers could come to our home so we could return their deposits.

A few years before the fire, after all the years living above the store, we built a very beautiful eight-room house with living quarters in the basement and were fixing it up slowly. Izz had his own den with special lights and built to his exact specifications. But after the fire, we decided to move to Toronto or somewhere close to see if we could establish a new life and new business and in a Jewish atmosphere for our children.

We left Rouyn–Noranda for Toronto on July 9, 1949 with a trailer attached to the car. I will never forget that day as long as I live. When our trailer detached itself from the car and everything we owned spilled onto the highway, I did not stop crying until 4 AM the next morning.

Commuting to Rouyn–Noranda

WE BEGAN THE PROCESS of looking for a new home and new

Rouyn street scene showing the still-smoking fire.

business in Toronto and in many towns and villages around the city. But everyone wanted an enormous amount of money which we did not have. So, we decided to go back to Rouyn–Noranda and build again since our name — Betty's Style Shop — and reputation were so well known, almost like the T. Eaton Company in Toronto. So, after we moved into a house in Toronto so the children could start school on September 1, 1949, Izz returned to Rouyn to build a new store at our location on 67 Main Street which was one of the best locations in town.

Our good reputation saved us. We needed a $40,000 loan from a trust company to start building, however the trust company said they would loan us $80,000 but only after the building and roof were complete. We did not have a lot of time to spare.

There was a new manager at the Canadian National Bank who reviewed our banking history with the Canadian National Bank and concluded that we should get the loan and did not see how the Trust Company refused us the $40,000 loan. He took it upon himself to write to the head office in Montreal to recommend our loan application be approved. To our astonishment and joy, it was.

In a few weeks we received $40,000 and Izz started to build. All through the winter he stood outside day after day, in forty below zero, supervising the building (and in many cases, personally correcting the mistakes of the architect and carpenters). By the end of May 1950, the building was finished.

Izz and I decided that we would like to open the store on August 17, on the same day that we had started the business many years before. We went around to Montreal and Toronto placing orders for merchandise. By the end of June, I came to Rouyn again with our two youngest children Susan and Debbie (who was eighteen months). Our two oldest girls, Lamie and Bunny were at Camp Shalom for the summer. We worked every day fixing up the store for the opening and I did this while taking care of two small children.

The Accident and the Store Opening

Two NIGHTS BEFORE the grand opening of the store there was a meeting at the synagogue that we both attended. We were living in a little apartment above the store that Izz built. Izz had to walk the baby sitter home which does not take very long. After a while when he did not return, I began to worry and suddenly, I heard footsteps coming up the stairs. It was the young man who had hit Izz. He said: Do not worry, he is alive, but I hit his leg and we must take him to the hospital to have an x-ray. We went to the hospital, but they had to keep him there for three or four days to treat him before they could put a cast on him.

I had to open the store on August 17 without Izz. I will never forget that day. I wanted so much for Izz to be there because he was the one that built it, but who are we to say what we want. We had designed a very modern store with two cash registers — one on the main floor and one in the basement. I had not bothered to learn how to use them because I depended on Izz for that and now, he was not there. When I went to open the doors, my eyes were filled with tears. It was a cloudy day and overcast at the time. I saw a lot of people standing outside but

Seventeen Is Fateful Number
For Owner of New Betty's Store

★ Seventeen is a significant number in the life of Irving Sherman, who will Thursday open his new store on Main Street.

First, he came to Rouyn on March 17, 1933. His building was burned on the same day, March 17, last year. He will be reopening on August 17, and one of his employees, Mrs. M. B. Chappelle, has been with him 17 years.

The new building includes two stores on the main floor with three offices and five apartments on the second.

Mr. Sherman believes that "pleasing the public has been responsible for my success."

Began With 33 Dresses

When he came to Rouyn he started in a second-floor room on Perrault street "with a trunk containing 33 dresses. A few weeks later he rented a store. In 1936 he moved to Main street and in 1941 he bought the building.

But his luck has not all been good. A week ago last Saturday he was struck by a car on the street and his leg was broken. On Thursday when his new building is officially opened he will have to enjoy it as best he can from a bed in the Youville Hospital.

The Rouyn–Noranda Press ran a story about Izz Sherman's accident, along with photos of the Sherman's newly-built Style Shoppe and the old fire-ravaged building. The store reopened in August 1950.

WATCH FOR OPENING ANNOUNCEMENT IN TUES. PAPER **BETTY'S** *Style* **SHOPPE** RE-OPENS THURSDAY, AUGUST 17th

assumed they were waiting for the bus which stopped in front of the store. We had advertised the store grand opening of course and our staff were all ready for the opening day.

Suddenly, the clouds dispersed and beautiful sunshine streamed through the windows into our store. People started to come in and before they looked at merchandise or anything else they came over to shake hands with me and tell us how happy they were that we were back and how they had missed us. It did not matter whether they

bought something or not. People just wanted to talk to us and express their happiness. Then bouquets of flowers started to arrive from the wholesalers. My heart expanded with happiness once again. I only felt bad that Izz was not there to experience this gracious welcome that they gave us that day.

So, we were in business again. Once Izz recovered, I left for Toronto with the children so they could start their new school in September. We lived in Toronto and Izz spent most of his time in Rouyn. He was in Rouyn for two to three weeks at a time and came to Toronto for a week or just a few days. At Christmas time and around Easter I would go up to Rouyn for about a month to help in the store. During the year when I could get someone to stay with the children, I also would go up north to give a helping hand in the store. §

THE NORTHERN DAILY NEWS

Pioneer Kirkland Lake Family Marks Mother's Birthday

One of Kirkland Lake's oldest residents, Mrs. Fanny Scott, celebrated her 70th birthday with a family dinner at the Park Lane Hotel, Sunday, March 23. Grouped around Mrs. Scott in the above picture is her immediate family, left to right, Mr. and Mrs. J. Scott, Mrs. H. Simons, Mrs. F. Scott and Mr. and Mrs. Louis Scott of Noranda. Back row, Harry Simmons and Mr. and Mrs. H. R. Scott.—Photo by Eddie Duke.

Louis & Norma Scott, seen in front row at right in this photograph, were among Rouyn–Noranda's early pioneers, and pillars of the Jewish community until they moved to Montreal in 1965. They are shown at a 70th birthday party in Kirkland Lake for Louis's mother. Northern Daily News, March 23, 1947.

Louis Scott, Rouyn–Noranda Pioneer
Obituary from Rouyn-Noranda Monitor (1973)

LOUIS SCOTT was reportedly one of the first people to settle in Rouyn–Noranda. His obituary, published in the *Rouyn–Noranda Monitor* in early 1973, gives a good sketch of his life:

"On Saturday, December 30th, 1972, at the Maimonides Hospital in Montreal, at the age of 74 and after a long illness, Louis Scott, one of Rouyn–Noranda's earliest pioneers, came to final rest.

Louis Scott, Pioneer Of 1924, Formed First Lumber Co. Here

1951

LOUIS SCOTT

This is the 23rd of a special series of articles on notable pioneers of Rouyn, whose 'exploits will be commemorated during the town's 25th anniversary celebrations next month.

By MIKE BOLTON

When Louis Scott arrived in Rouyn in December, 1924, there was plenty of land for sale for building sites, but the main difficulty facing prospective buyers was travelling through the deep snow to their location. Mr. Scott remembers that Nelson Pinder used to solve this problem by lending his clients a pair of snowshoes.

In the spring, when the snow had left the ground, he remembers that it was necessary to walk to and from Macamic for business trips.

The other mode of transportation, which he used occasionally, was an old army airplane which flew from Rouyn to Haileybury. It carried two passengers, but the cockpits were uncovered.

Imaginary Streets

At first firewood was no problem. According to Mr. Scott the early settlers just chopped it from their own lots, or from the bush in front of the property, which eventually became a road. At that time the site of the present city of Rouyn was covered with a luxurious blanket of spruce, jack-pine, birch and tamarack. Streets were just an imaginary line through the bush.

When he first arrived here Mr. Scott took part in building, clearing and ditching the first mile of the Macamic highway.

"After that, not having much to do," said Mr. Scott, "I gathered, 10 car-loads of empty beer bottles, which were of no value at that time, but brought a considerable amount of money when the railroad came in. Then I lost the beer bottle money in a bad invest-

great importance but, was able to make a few deals."

Faith In Future

"Most of us oldtimers had great faith in the future of the Twin Cities and vicinity," declared Mr. Scott. "Looking back to the area's insignificant bgeinning, and to the transformation into the important mining centre of today we see that our faith was justified."

Speaking of the present, he said: "The apparent indifferent attitude of the federal government towards gold mining has greatly retarded the future growth of this country.

"But I feel sure that in time they will see that the importance of our mineral wealth merits revision of this attitude. I feel sure this district will grow, and continue to be, one of the most important mining centres of our country."

"Operating Scott's Drug Sundries on 8th Street in Noranda in the early thirties, Louis Scott became a popular and well-known figure in the Twin Cities, by reason of his affability, his joviality, and his recognized integrity. Completely bilingual, he was respected and admired by all elements in the community, the foreign-born as well as English and French.

"In the late forties he organized the Rouyn Metal Company Ltd. and conducted this operation successfully until 1965 when, for reasons of deteriorating health, he and Mrs. Scott moved to Montreal.

"An ardent bridge player, he and his wife (nee Koza) of Cobalt were enthusiastic members of the Rouyn–Noranda Duplicate Bridge Club. A member of the local Kneseth Israel Congregation, he served a term as president.

"Representing one of the few remaining links between the present generation and the original settlers of this area, the death of Louis Scott is being widely mourned by his numerous friends and by the many hundreds of others who knew him.

"He is survived by his wife Norma, who originates from Cobalt, Ontario, his brothers Ruby, Kirkland Lake and Joe, Toronto, his sister Mrs. Sonia Simons, Florida, a daughter, Sally (Mrs. Eli Fagen) and a daughter, Sylvia (Mrs. Bert Sauer) as well as five grandchildren." §

Noranda,Que.
Feb.5yh.1957.

Dear Zelda.
        As you see I am back in Noranda and at the office again.
Louis left on Sunday for Montreal and from there on to Rochester,
and the clinic.I expect him to be away at least two weeks,and I hope
that he will return with a clean bill of health and feel the better
for having gone.
        I was very happy to have been able to see you and Sam and
the children even for a rt while,and am only sorry that e could
not get to-gether for a real heart to heart talk as we used to do.
That is something that I miss very much and something that I need,
very much,but I suppose one has to do the best one can in life.
        Sylvia is feeling fine and so am I,however I have been so tied
up at the office that I haven't seen a soul since I returned from
Toronto.Rae Mednick told me that you spoke to her on the phone and
therefore you must know the little news that there is here if any.
Things are very quiet here and the only news I have heard is that
Becky Ritter has gone to Montreal for a visit.Shephoned me that she
was leaving and if I wished her to call Sally,I told her to do so if
she wished,so I will hear the results when she returns.
        Tamal is having the Hadassah meeting at her home to-morrow
evening,and they will probably discuss the card party that is to take
place on the 27th.of this month.I wonder what kind of success we will
have this year.Perhaps we will be surprised and we will make a lot
of money,but I doubt it.However time will tell.
        How is everything with you Zelda? and have you come to a
decision about moving or selling your new home ? whatever you decide
I hope you will be very happy.How was Bess's anniversay party?I forgot
completely that it was to take place on the 3rd.I hear that my sister
Becky has been in bed again,so I haven't received any letters from her.
        Well Zelda,dear friend,I believe I have written you all there
was to write.Take care of yourself and keep well and happy,with best
wishes and love to you,Sam and the children.I remain,as always with love
                                        Norma. Scott

Typed letter from Norma Scott to Zelda
Mednick, Noranda, 1957.

Mike (Motel) Smith with Esther Sandberg.

Mike Smith: Finding A New Family in the North
by Ellen Smith (his wife)

I AM A TORONTONIAN who met Mike Smith in 1968. I was working at the Montreal General and Mike was in Montreal on a business trip. Unfortunately, I do not have northern roots and while Mike was living in Noranda (beginning about 1948) I believe he had rooms in various boarding houses . . . but was well fed by the Jewish families of his friends.

Mike (Motel) Smith (originally Schmidaka) had been an officer in the Russian Army during World War Two. He was a scout. Scouts worked mostly at night behind enemy lines. With the help of the partisans, they would find and destroy German positions. Mike had no family in Canada. Almost all of his family had died in the Holocaust. Mike escaped to Germany and as a Displaced Person was offered employment as a lumberjack in Canada. He arrived in Halifax on September 13, 1947 and was assigned to a lumber camp in Kapuskasing, Ontario.

In Kapuskasing he met a Jewish businessman, Harry Farb.

Harry told Ed Gold, a Jewish salesman from Toronto, about the young Jewish lumberjack from Russia. Ed Gold, in turn, told his friend in Rouyn–Noranda, Sidney Sandberg, about this strange newcomer. Sidney was excited and immediately arranged for Mike to travel by train to Rouyn–Noranda so they could meet. As Sidney expected, Motel was a relative, a cousin from his mother's side. Indeed, he had been at Motel's *bris* in 1923.

After Mike completed his brief commitment as a lumberjack (he was not sufficiently skilled), he moved to Rouyn–Noranda and was hired by Noranda Mines. His job was to climb the ladder outside the smokestack to assess the mineral deposit at the top. He worked there for five years.

While he was generally known and accepted by the larger northern Jewish community, he became particularly close friends with the Sandberg, Korman, Martin and Mednick families.

In 1953 he moved to Toronto. At first he worked in construction. With improved language skills, he started his own business — M. Smith Sales. He remained in touch with his northern pals as many of the younger generation had also moved south.

In 1967 he became an owner of Grays Department Store in Windsor, Ontario. He remained as proprietor until 1989 when the property was purchased by a bank. He returned to M. Smith Sales and was active in business until he retired in 2020 at the age of ninety-seven. He always maintained close connections with the northern Jewish community that had befriended him as a young Yiddish-speaking immigrant. §

Above, Rose & Benjamin Zifkin. At right, Benjamin
Zifkin in the mine, 1400 feet under the ground.

A Bit of My Zifkin Ancestry
by David Zifkin

AS THE LAST SURVIVING MEMBER of my family, I no longer have the ability to reach out to my sister Anita, who recently passed away, and who knew much more of the family history than I. In previous years I would also speak to my Aunt Fannie, my father's sister, who was a valuable source of information.

Unfortunately, I have no recollection of my Zaida Benjamin who died when I was about five years old. The few details I know are as follows:

My grandfather, Benjamin Zifkin, was born in Pochep in Moghilev Gubernia (now in Bryansk) in 1887. His father, David Zifkin, was a rabbi; I was named after him.

He came from a family of eleven children. He served in the Russian army for seven years and was the photographer to the Czar. He came to Canada with my grandmother, Rose, in 1913 on the ship *Andania*.

I don't know when he came to Noranda; however, my grandparents must have left Noranda in 1951, since they purchased a house in Toronto in November 1951. §

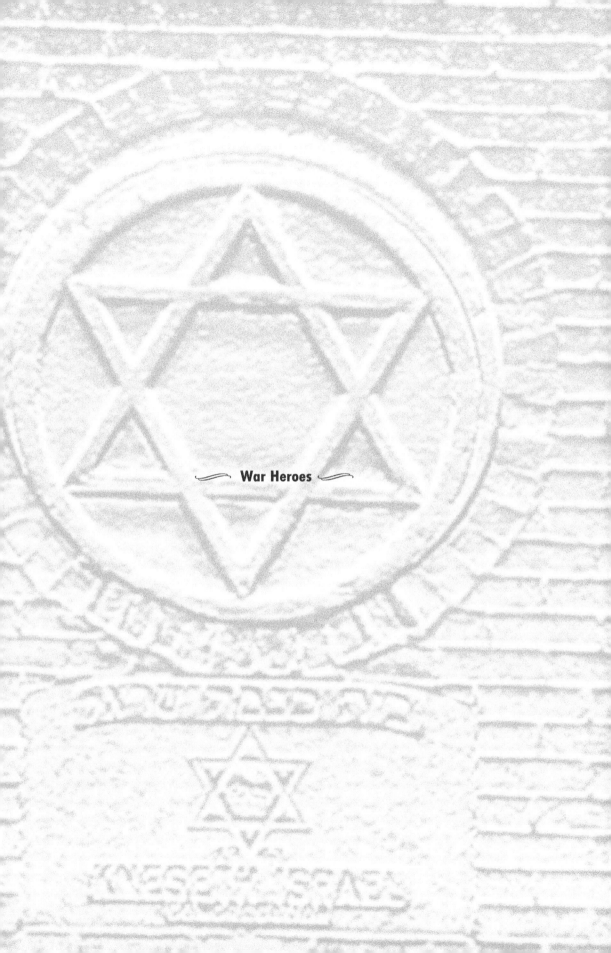

— War Heroes —

A Life of Extreme Joys and Profound Sorrows
by Steve Arnold (from the Hamilton Spectator, November 18, 2012)

I T WAS HARRY KORMAN'S smile that struck you first, an ear-to-ear grin that split his face like a chevron.

He had a lot to smile about. A successful business career, a 47-year marriage, two children, four grandchildren and a wide circle of friends in the Shriners, the Masonic Lodge, his synagogue.

That was the life Harry Korman left on October 22 at the age of seventy-nine.

Before those happy years, however, there was another life in another world, under other names. A life where a nine-year-old boy named Chaskel Bernstein saw his father shot down in the street and his neighbours herded into a ghetto to die of hunger and disease or to be shipped off to a death factory.

A world where a thirteen-year-old child soldier called Julius Rupp could machine gun nine men and then calmly take an accordion from one of the bodies and teach himself to play.

Harry Korman was born Chaskel Bernstein in 1932 in Stanislawow, a provincial capital in southeastern Poland. In a video interview before illness locked his memories away forever, he told his story for the benefit of his children, grandchildren and history.

He lived "a normal kid's life" filled with school, soccer and friends, parents, Sam and Sally, and sister, Natasha.

That all changed between 1939 and 1941, when first the Russians and then the Germans swept over Stanislawow. It was during that second invasion that Sam was killed and Sally and Natasha fled deep into Russia.

"He was fighting right around our home," Korman recalled. "A neighbour took me away to the bush. There was a lot of people there.

"To me it was all like a game. I didn't realize my father was dead, I just took it like a big game. Maybe it was good I took it like that. After that everything moved pretty fast."

For eighteen months, the young boy lived in the forest with a group of other refugees, emerging at night to seek food and "to do some damage to the Germans if they could."

Much of that sabotage was planned around information ten-year-old Chaskel gathered by brazenly walking the streets of Stanislawow, protected only by the disregard German guards paid a child.

"It was still a game to me," he said. "I would look around for things like where were soldiers sleeping, how big a force they had, did they have any tanks? Just anything that would be interesting to somebody fighting them. I wasn't afraid because it was all still a game."

After eighteen months, the tide of war turned and the Germans retreated in the face of an avenging Red Army. Chaskel and his sister, by then a nurse in a Czech army unit attached to the Russians, were reunited. Young Chaskel joined them to be near his sister and was taken under the wing of a Czech officer named Rupp. He took the name Julius Rupp and gained a reputation as a fierce warrior.

In one incident, as the Soviets waged bitter street-by-street, house-by-house battles through Prague, a thirteen-year-old Rupp

Photo taken on the day that Chaskel received his decoration from both the Polish and Czech governments. Chaskel, the youngest decorated soldier, stands beside the oldest decorated soldier. Behind Chaskel is his sister Natasha (Bernstein) Adamek and husband Victor Adamek.

ducked into an apartment building and while groping in the dark grabbed a live wire. The resulting shock knocked him out.

"When I woke up it was quiet, there was no more street fighting," he recalled. "I opened the door and there were nine Germans. They were just resting, they thought the war had passed them by.

"I took my machine gun and just sprayed bullets at them," he said. "I felt okay about that. I didn't feel anything bad. We were there to shoot Germans, so what the hell?"

From the body of one he took an accordion, and taught himself to play. He still had that instrument in 1948, when he landed in Halifax.

As he had for the Polish partisans, young Rupp served as a frontline spy, gathering the information that would be used to plan future attacks. It was on one of those missions that he was captured.

He told that story to the *Canadian Jewish Chronicle* in 1948. Tortured by the SS into giving up the location of his unit, he instead led 120 Germans into an ambush.

In 1948, at age fifteen, Chaskel Bernstein, his sister and her husband came to Canada. Chaskel was adopted by Joe and Shaindel

Korman. They had successful businesses, but no children.

Under his new name of Harry Korman, the former boy soldier helped run those enterprises, played music with the likes of Ronnie Hawkins and Levon Helm, palled around with hockey great Dave Keon, married at age thirty-two and started a family.

In the eulogy he delivered at Korman's funeral, grand-nephew David Halporn grasped for the meaning of a life filled with such extremes of tragedy and happiness.

"How can we explain this? That our Harry came out of that black hole not bitter and hardened, but hopeful and tender and kind?" he asked. "That was his spark and the tragedies of his youth simply could not put it out."

For Chaskel Bernstein, aka Julius Rupp aka Harry Korman, the fact he survived at all could only be explained by the Yiddish word "bashert" — fate.

"It was just strictly bashert that I survived," he said at the end of his recorded interview. "It was just meant to be. I wasn't a particularly good man that I should live. I was a normal man, but when something good happens you just have to be thankful for it." §

Isaac Korman D.F.C, Canadian War Hero
by Esther (Korman) Verred

MY FATHER, ISAAC KORMAN, travelled to North Bay on August 29, 1941, at the age of twenty, and enlisted in the Canadian Armed Forces for World War Two. He received his training in Regina and Toronto as a bombardier-navigator-gunner and graduated on August 4, 1942. After a brief holiday back in Noranda, he was shipped to England in October 1942.

During the war he made thirty-three flights over Germany with RCAF squadron 158. Because of this, he was awarded the Distinguished Flying Cross personally by King George VI at Buckingham Palace on August 4, 1944. His citation reads:

> Warrant Officer Korman has completed a notable tour during which he has taken part in several attacks on the German capital and many other in the Ruhr area. He is a most determined and gallant member of aircraft crew and his successes are an excellent testimony to the accuracy of his bombing. His conduct at all times has been exemplary.

My father arrived back from England on January 5, 1945, where

Welcome Party for Isaac Korman upon his return from ww2 deployment in England. Rouyn–Noranda Train Station, January 5, 1945.

❧ Front row (children), left to right: Stanley Pekelis, Julian (Yudel) Kitty, Murray Rice, Henry Korman, Shlaime (Saul) Korman, Isaac Korman, Willie Korman, Faye (Sandberg) Goldfarb, Howard Luke, Marlene Luke, Marsha (Sandberg) Feldman.

❧ Middle row, left to right: Lazar Kitty, Mrs Luke, Sonya Korman (wife of Nachman), Rae (Korman) Rice, Temel Korman, Dvosha Korman (wife of Simcha Korman), Esther (Korman) Sandberg, Sonny Korman.

❧ Back row, left to right: Frank Cohen, Sam (Simcha) Korman (son of David), Joe Korman, Simcha Korman (brother of Temel Korman), Rose (Miller) Korman, Michel Korman, Isaac Korman (son of Michel and Temel), Fanny (Korman) Weinstein (daughter of Michel and Temel Korman), Sidney Sandberg, Jack Korman, Morris Pekilis.

he was greeted at the train station by family and friends. It was a very momentous day for all the Jews of Rouyn–Noranda. Isaac retired from the RCAF on April 11, 1945. He and my mother, Rose Miller, were married on July 22, 1945. §

Also Served

- Lionel Clare, Royal Canadian Airforce
- Victor Finkelman, Royal Canadian Airforce
- Mair Katz, Royal Highland Regiment
- Sam Korman, Canadian Armed Forces
- Mike Smith, Officer in the Russian Army
- Harry Miller, Reserves

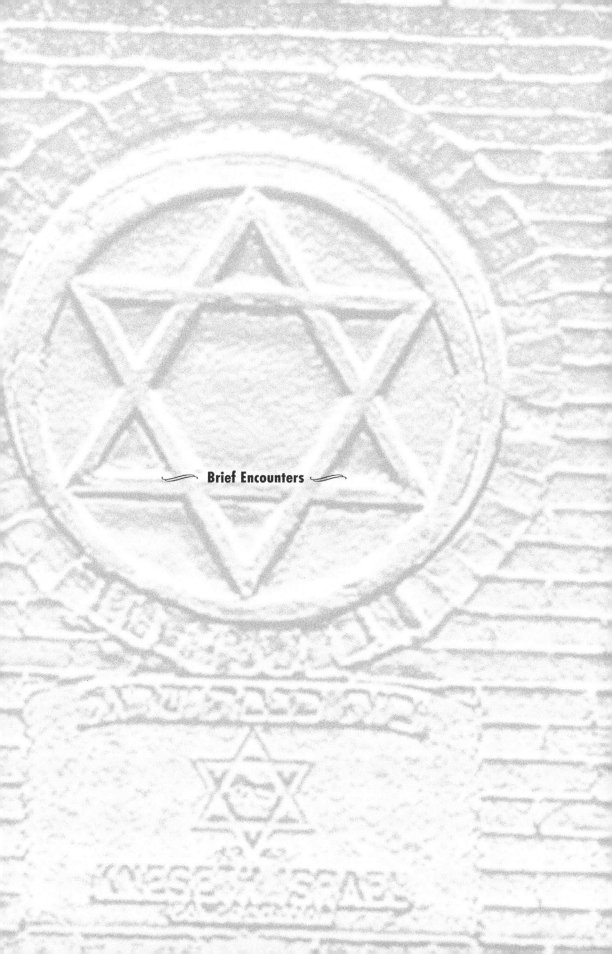

~ **Brief Encounters** ~

A Memorable Interlude in Rouyn–Noranda

by Robert Cohen

I WAS BORN AND RAISED IN VANCOUVER BC and studied Mining & Mineral Process Engineering at UBC just as my father and brother had done; we graduated in 1949, 1978 and 1992 respectively. In 1991 I worked a summer job at the Macassa Mine in Kirkland Lake, Ontario and in 1992 I worked at a mine in Chile. While looking for my first full time employment in early 1993, I interviewed with Lac Minerals in Toronto. While they didn't have a full-time job available at the time, they did have an opportunity to work at their Doyon Mine outside of Rouyn near the town of Cadillac.

I was eager for work experience and jumped on the opportunity, arriving in Rouyn–Noranda on February 13, 1993, a freezing cold day. Having come from Vancouver, I didn't know what cold was until coming to Rouyn–Noranda. I found a rooming house to live in at 95 – 14th Street. It was adequate and comfortable; however, I was lacking a car. I was in a car pool to go to and from the mine, but had to walk everywhere while in town.

I made a few friends, mostly from colleagues at the mine and others nearby. On Saturday nights we'd head to the O'Toole bar in Rouyn and have a few beers, play darts and chat. Funny enough, once in awhile I would recognize a few Kirkland Lakers who would pop into town for a change of scenery from the Kirkland Lake scene. It was always nice to have a few anglophones to chat with as my command of the French language, while adequate, was far from perfect.

One night after the bar closed at O'Tooles a few of us got into a car to drive to Noranda for some late night poutine at Chez Morasse Poutine. (Chez Morasse Poutine is a very popular diner, located at 9th Street and Murdoch in the building that once was Noranda Bread.) Along the way, looking out the car window, I noticed what appeared to be a synagogue but, being dark out, I couldn't be sure.

The next day I set out by foot to verify what I had seen — and *voila*, it was indeed a synagogue, but now obviously converted to an apartment block. Having worked in Kirkland Lake, I saw the same outcome with their synagogue there, so what I was seeing did not surprise me. I saw the cornerstone block laid by Michel Korman in 1949 and the Beit Kneseth Israel sign in Hebrew from 1948 over the front door below the round window with blue-stained glass showing a Magen David. Nevertheless, I was dismayed at seeing a well-painted white swastika to the left of the cornerstone, another smaller one over the cornerstone itself, and *"Guerre aux Juifs"* spray-painted on the side of the building. Whoever did this, I thought, probably had never even met a Jew, and it was beyond me to understand why they must have felt so wronged by a Jew.

In the weeks that followed, I would walk by and notice that the graffiti was still present. I wondered why the landlord and the tenants just let it be there. Following that, I was at the mine, having a casual conversation at work with one of my colleagues. He asked me about my last name and asked if I was Jewish. He told me that there was once a Jewish community in town and if I knew that there was an old synagogue still in town. When I told him that indeed I was aware, I told him that I was dismayed by the anti-semitic graffiti on the building and that it wasn't being removed. He looked at me and told me, "My friend is the mayor; I will have this looked after immediately!" And sure enough it was. Within a few days it was removed. It wasn't a perfect removal job, but it was removed nonetheless.

In 1998, a handful of years later, I moved to Toronto to work as a mutual fund manager, specializing in mining stocks. Once again, I was moving to a new town after having spent over three years working in Chile and Australia and a couple of years working in a corporate office of a mining company in Vancouver. As I expanded my network of new friends, hapchance one of them introduced me to Sol Mednick. After meeting Sol and chatting for a while, he mentioned that he grew up in Rouyn–Noranda. When I told him that I had spent some time living there in 1993 he nearly fell off his chair! He couldn't believe that a Jew went there, he thought they only came from there! As we got to know each other better we both learned that his folks and my grandmother hail from the same shtetl, David–Horodok, in what is now Belarus. Many David–Horodokers wound up in Michigan and some in Winnipeg, but a few, such as the Mednicks and the Muroffs, ventured to Rouyn–Noranda. Interestingly, members of Sol's family recognized my grandmother's family name — Kaluzny — bearers of which wound up in both Detroit and Winnipeg. So years later, I learned that the members that founded Kneseth Israel in Rouyn–Noranda have a much closer family connection than I would have ever guessed way back when I was twenty-four years old and working there.

As a side note, in 1997 I met another Jewish fellow from Montreal, Maor Amar, who did his undergrad in mining engineering at McGill. He also lived in Rouyn–Noranda in the mid-1990s working for Inmet. He was then courting Myriam Kiperman, the woman who later became his wife; she even came up to Rouyn–Noranda to visit him there! §

Jack Stoch

Recollections of a Jewish Mining Executive
by Jack Stoch

WHEN I FIRST ARRIVED in Rouyn–Noranda in 1972, there were few Jews left and certainly no active synagogue. I became friends with the Garmaise family and met Max Martin occasionally; I also interacted occasionally with a geologist, Joel Scodnick, when he was based there.

I worked for Noranda Exploration for about two and a half years, doing a lot of field work, so I was in and out of town and didn't get an opportunity to interact to any serious degree with what little Jewish community remained. I quit Noranda Exploration and I started doing consulting and property acquisitions to the point that the mines ministry said that I was the largest private mineral rights holder in Quebec.

In 1987 I listed a public exploration company called Globex Mining Enterprises Inc. on the Montreal stock exchange. Several years later we listed on exchanges in Toronto, the United States, Germany and various others. We started off with one property and now have over 200 exploration assets including 80 royalties principally in Eastern Canada. We work in Eastern Canada, the United States and

Saxony Germany. We will shortly be expanding our reach to Portugal once we receive our final permits.

Met a lady over forty years ago who transferred up to Rouyn–Noranda to perfect smelter accounting, Dianne Jarvis. She was coming up for a two-year stint but we hit it off and got married. She eventually quit Noranda Mines and came to work with me at Globex as secretary treasurer until her retirement. Her two years turned into thirty-five years in Rouyn–Noranda. Our friends were and are almost all professionals so eventually they all moved along with their families to other cities and countries.

After thirty-five years Dianne got fed up and said we had to re-establish our roots in the Toronto area where we both have family. We did but maintained two residences, one in Toronto and one on Lac Dufault. All Globex's staff lived and live in the Rouyn–Noranda area and I go back and forth splitting my time between the two towns. We are currently opening a permanent office in Toronto. I continue to work for Globex as president and CEO. And we continue to grow from a junior exploration company to a profitable diversified exploration and royalty company. This is a novelty in the junior exploration space as few companies have a long life and make a profit. §

Jack Weinstein,
circa 1963

Dedicated to Jack Weinstein
by Bernadine (Miller) Harrar

JACK WEINSTEIN WAS a first cousin to Esther and Jerry Korman, and a second cousin to Harvey, Kathy and Sidney Korman. He was the son of Eddie and Fanny Weinstein and the grandson of Michel and Temel Korman. He was a year older than me and was an integral part of my gang. He was the nicest guy you could ever meet and everybody loved him. Jack was born in Noranda in 1946 and moved to North Bay with his family when he was seven years old, but came back to spend summers with us. He lived in Noranda for one school year when we were teenagers and attended the Noranda High School. He participated in all of our activities. He was even the manager for the Wild Cats, the band that Harvey was a part of.

Then, in his mid teens, he moved to Montreal for good. Afterwards, we really missed him. True to his word, he returned to stay the summer with us. This time he returned with two very good Jewish male friends, Jack Kligman and Mark Buchwald. So, as it turned out, Esther and I had "imported" Jewish boyfriends for a little while that year. It was very interesting! We showed them all the sights. We took them to our cabin at Lake Dufault. We figured that Montrealers are not very hardy because they couldn't run barefoot on the gravel at Dufault, like we could.

Jack invited us to Montreal the following Christmas holidays. Many of us took the bus and spent a memorable week with him. We learned to navigate the buses and we met his new friends. For most of us, it was our first time without parents in the big city. Most of us moved to Montreal to go to McGill or, in my case, to nursing school. Jack would organize outings for hockey games. He knew the schedule of the games for the farm team of the Montreal Canadiens. For one dollar we would buy standing room tickets to their games at the Forum. We knew a lot of the players because my brother, Marvin, had played minor hockey with them.

In Montreal, Jack worked for the Frieds in their meat packing plant. So when I wanted to make a big meat order, I would coordinate it with Jack. He made sure that I got good service and special cuts of meat. He was an important link for me in integrating into Montreal life.

Jack became ill and died just before Covid. His wife, Brenda, has become a part of our "gang." Rest in peace, Jack. We miss you. §

Honourable Mentions

The Caplan Family. David and Ida Caplan came to Canada about 1900 and lived in Toronto before arriving in Rouyn–Noranda in the mid-1920s, among the earliest Jews to settle there. Although David may have continued to work as a butcher as he had done in Toronto, he likely also had business interests that brought him to the northern mining town. The couple may have maintained two residences at first; there is no evidence that any of their seven children lived in Rouyn–Noranda for any significant period. Ida died in Rouyn–Noranda in 1934 and was buried in Toronto. David remarried in 1937; the marriage record describes him as a merchant living at 366 Perrault Street, Rouyn. He died in Rouyn in 1941 and was buried in Toronto.

Cohen snack bar

Frank & Olga Cohen lived on 9th Street. Frank was an umpire for the Rouyn–Noranda baseball league and operated a small snack bar at the baseball diamond. He also owned a smoke shop.

Sorel Crotin

Sorel (Korman) Crotin was brought to Noranda by her brother Simcha Korman and arrived in Canada from Horodyshche, Russia, in 1930; she was also a sister to Temel Korman and to Joe (Yossel) Korman. She worked in a factory in Toronto for a while, and later returned to Rouyn–Noranda. Shortly after, on March 19, 1933 she married Walter Crotin from Ansonville and set up residence in Ansonville. Their wedding was the first in the original Rouyn–Noranda synagogue. They have two children, Manny Crotin and Fagel (Crotin) Mendelson.

Reverend Diamond was a spiritual leader who taught cheder and bar mitzvah.

Abraham Duke, a photographer, his wife, Leah, and son, Morris, arrived from Ukraine in 1913. They lived in Quebec City and then La Tuque, and had a slot machine business in Northern Quebec. With the arrival of Ethel, Eddie, Dave, and Sylvia, they moved to Val d'Or and then Rouyn–Noranda in the mid-1930s. A few years later they moved to Kirkland Lake where Abraham finally opened a photography studio with his sons.

Harry (Chaim) Farber was Zelda Mednick's brother. Sam Mednick, Zelda's husband, through lots of time, money and phone calls, was able to obtain a visa for Harry to leave the UNRRA camp in Italy after WW2, and get him into Canada. He worked in Sam Mednick's grocery store in Noranda for about a year before moving to Toronto to open his own grocery store. Later, Chaim and Sam Mednick started a company called Torno (Toronto–Noranda) that built homes and rental apartment buildings.

Mr. Fogel was in the blueberry business with a small warehouse on Mercier Street near Gamble Street in Noranda. "We used to sell him our blueberries when Mr. Muravsky, who had a small grocery next door to him, drove us out in the morning to pick blueberries in the hills on the north side of Noranda," recalled Dr. Isaac Katz.

Mr. Ginsberg was a butcher and cattle dealer. He and his family spent about twenty-five years in Noranda. After his family moved to Montreal, he continued to come back to Noranda for several summers to engage in the cattle business.

Izzie & Dora Gold lived in Noranda with two sons for a short while. Mr. Gold was in the insurance business. The family moved to Cleveland in the 1950s.

Mr. and Mrs. Goldiner. Mr. Goldiner was a cheder teacher for one year in the late 1950s.

The Hager Family. Mrs. Hager had a ladies store on Main Street in Rouyn. She moved to Montreal and her daughter Elizabeth Hager had an upscale ladies store in the Cavendish Mall and later, on Queen Mary Road in Montreal.

Lazar Kitty had a soft soda company called Kitty's Kik. Mrs. Kitty ran a small grocery store on Main Street next to Ansara Clothing store. They were married in Montreal in 1932 and a had a son named Julius (Yudel).

A.M. Klein. Mr. Klein, the well-known Canadian writer and poet, practiced law in Rouyn–Noranda with Max Garmaise for a few years starting in 1935. (*See Garmaise story.*)

Joe (Yossel) Korman, brother to Sorel (Korman) Crotin and Simcha Korman, was brought to Canada by his other sister Temel Korman. He arrived in Rouyn–Noranda from Horodyshche, Russia, in the late 1920s. He initially lived with his sister and brother-in-law, Temel and Michel Korman, and worked as a junk and scrap metal dealer in Noranda. On August 10, 1941 he married Regina Simak and moved to Montreal where he became a tool and die maker, working for Pratt & Whitney.

Benny & Shaifel Korson escaped Kiev during turbulent times before World War Two and made their way to Montreal where they lived for a number of years. They moved to Rouyn–Noranda in 1943 and opened a confectionery store. Their daughter and son-in-law, **Nelly & Lou Revzen**, followed them to Rouyn–Noranda. Lou was the president of the local branch of B'nai Brith and had a butcher shop. The Revzens had two children born in Noranda, Helene and Barry. The Korsons and the Revzens moved to Toronto in 1948. The Revzens had another daughter, Marissa, born in Toronto.

Denise (Denny) Loeb. Denny Loeb from Winnipeg lived in Noranda for a couple of years in the mid-1950s and worked in the office of Waite Amulet Mines. She lived with Norma and Harry Miller, her sister and brother-in-law, while she was here. She left when she met and married Zol Pinsk of Winnipeg.

The Luke Family operated Luke's Menswear in Rouyn. Isaac and Rose (Schwartz) Luke were married in Cobalt, Ontario in 1932, and had three children, Iris, Marlene and Howard. The family moved to Montreal while Mr. Luke continued to run his business in Rouyn.

Alter Chaim Mair Pollak, who lost his wife and two children in the Holocaust, was a nephew of the Katz and Fried families of Rouyn–Noranda; his mother, Chaya Sarah, was a sister to Gitel Fried and Golda Katz. Upon his release from the camps, he went to Sweden and contacted his relatives in Rouyn–Noranda, who

Rouyn-Noranda Press

· Mar 10, 1949

NEWCOMER IS HONOR GUEST

Mr. and Mrs Morris "Sam" Freid, Rouyn, entertained at the Synagogue on Sunday evening in honor of their nephew Maeir Pollak, who arrived about three week's ago in the twin cities from Sweden.

Most of the congregation was on hand to welcome Mr. Pollak into the community. Max Garmaise acted as master of ceremonies for the evening and called upon B Zifkin to render a few homeland songs, which he did with great ease and clearity, Michel Korman, president of the community then welcomed Mr. Pollack and invited him as a member. A visitor, Mr. Isenberg, of Toronto, was also called upon to say a few words. More folks songs were heard from Charlie Farber, followed by an impressive speech by Louis Revzen, president of the B'Nai B'Rith Club. Mr. Revzen expressed his hopes that Mr. Pollak would become a member of the local organization. On behalf of the Ladies' Hadassah, Mrs. S. Schlein extended the welcome. Sam Fried then addressed the gathering thanking all for attending and especially to the women who aided Mrs. Freid in serving the lunch. Mr. Pollak took the floor and with precise Hebrew extended warm and sincere thanks to his aunts and uncles, Mr. and Mrs. Freid and Rabbi and Mrs. Katz. He told of his life under the Hitler regime and compared it to the warm feeling that is found in Canada. He admires Canadians and hopes to be a "good citizen".

Mr. Pollak came to Canada from Sweden where he taught Hebrew in the colleges there. Previous to this he was a secretary at the town hall in Romania. He was forced into the German concentration camps, and there lost his wife and two children. At present he is engaged and hopes to bring his future wife to Canada. He is a very highly educated man.

sponsored him to come to Canada. He arrived in February 1949. As reported in the Rouyn–Noranda Press, there was a reception at the synagogue in Noranda to welcome him. He was in Rouyn–Noranda for a short time during which he was able to arrange for his fiancee, Toby Wiesel, a cousin of Elie Wiesel, to come to Canada. The Pollaks then moved to Montreal where they had two sons, Herschel and Yankel. Herschel married Chai Liba and lives in New York; they have eight children and numerous grandchildren. Yankel married Shaindy and raised five children in Montreal; they, too, have been blessed with numerous grandchildren.

Regina & Joe Korman, 1941.

Louis & Nelly (Korson) Revzen lived in Noranda and later moved to Toronto. (See the "Korson" entry for more details.)

Sunny Rice, daughter of Noranda pioneers Isaac and Rose Rice, left home at an early age and became a dancer on Broadway. She married a surgeon and lived in New York. She was featured with many leading bands, including the Dorsey Brothers and Artie Shaw. Sometimes, while visiting her family in Rouyn, she would perform at the Charlebois night club. Many of the Jewish residents as well as others would go to the evening show which was usually highly acclaimed.

Meyer Sharony

Meyer Sharony was a Hebrew teacher and spiritual leader for the Jewish community. He was a very learned man with a great voice who enjoyed teaching and singing songs. He certainly had an impact on the younger generation of Rouyn–Noranda Jewish youth. He is the teacher most often mentioned by contributors to this book. He died in Baycrest Hospital, Toronto.

Sy & Suzie Schlien

The Schlien Family. Sy & Suzie Schlien owned Capital Credit Jewellers in Rouyn. Their sons are Joey and David.

Charlie & Bert Steinberg operated a bowling alley in Noranda. Charlie left the town and his wife, Bert, remained and opened a deli restaurant in the New Townsite. He also had a used-car dealership. They had a daughter, Roz.

Capital Credit Jewellers

Mrs. Rose Stone was a photographer who had a photography

shop on Main Street near Perrault in Rouyn.

Mr. Teitelbaum had a fashionable clothing store on Perrault Street in Rouyn. He spent about twenty-five years in Rouyn and left after his wife passed away. He was very close to Rabbi Katz and the Katz family. The Rouyn telephone directory of 1926 lists Teitelbaum Ladies and Gents Furnishing on Perrault, phone 33.

The Weinstein Family. Eddie Weinstein & Fanny (nee Korman) were married in Rouyn–Noranda in 1945. Fanny was the daughter of Michel & Temel Korman, and Eddie worked for his father-in-law in Mike Korman's Menswear. Then they moved to North Bay and opened a clothing store. They had two children born in Noranda, Jack and Maury.

Rifka (Rita) and Voveh (William) Weinstein. Rifka was Jack Ritter's sister, whom he brought to Noranda after the war. They lived in Noranda briefly before moving to Montreal.

Nathan & Molly Wiesenthal had a grocery store on Main Street in Rouyn, called Main Food Market. The children were Julian, Marvin, Norman and Florence.

Mr. Wolovsky (or Volosky) is remembered by a number of former residents of Rouyn–Noranda who were children when they knew him. Some remember him as an occasional guest around their parents' or grandparents' Shabbos dinner table. A disabled man with misformed arms, he reportedly worked as a salesman for the Dexter Shoe Company, and travelled a lot. §

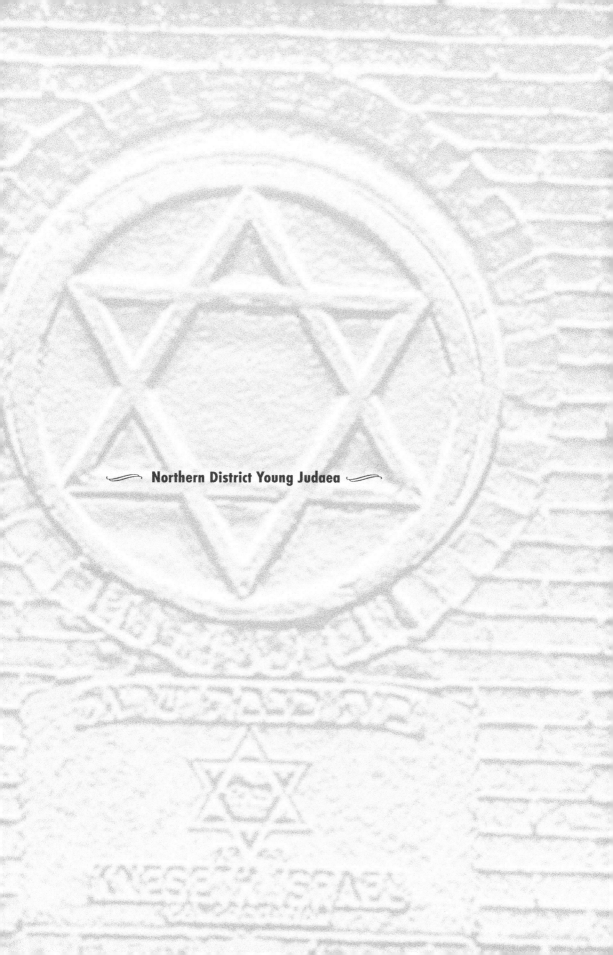

Northern District Young Judaea

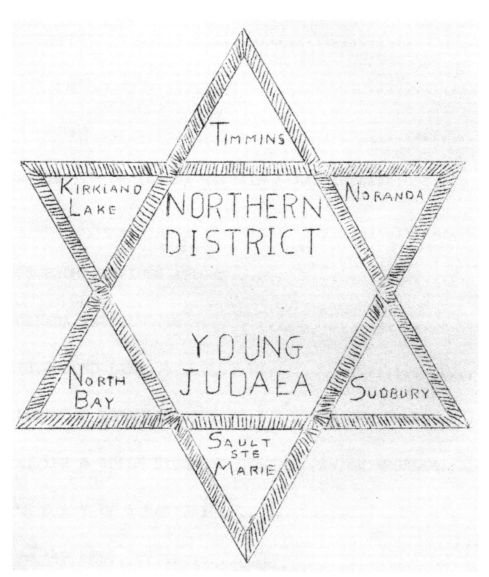

Young Judaea: An Immersion in Jewish Culture
by Rosalie (Mednick) Nepom

THANKS IN LARGE PART to the Northern District of Canadian Young Judaea, young people from Jewish families in Rouyn–Noranda were kept very busy. In addition to the regular sports and extracurricular activities that occurred during the school year, our lives were filled with Jewish activities throughout the year.

We believe that Young Judaea in Rouyn–Noranda was started by Shlomo Pekilis with assistance from Jack Korman (a student at the time), Sally Scott and Dolores Mednick, and also Young Judaea

Young Judaea Holds Northern Kinus

Pictured above are the 50 chaverim from the 5 centres of North Bay, Sudbury, Timmins, Kirkland Lake and Noranda who attended the recent successful Northern District Kinus.
Bottom row, left to right: Johnny Jessel, Bobby Maidenberg, Sandy Herman, Lu Steinberg, Mr. M. Garmaise, Ernie Abbit, Jerry Korman, Dave Hamburg, Mr. M. Sharony, Lorne Duke, Goldie Greenspoon, Lester Brown, Carolyn Shub.
Second row, left to right: Phyllis Brown, Rhoda Nemchin, Paula Gurvitch, Bernadine Miller, Esther Korman, Sherry Herman, Ronny Dash, Herman Koza, Linda Littman, Kathy Korman, Robby Jessel, David Garmaise, Harriet Abramson, Jack Wienstein, Stanley Herman, Harvey Korman, Laurie Miller.
Third row, left to right: George Getzler, Steve Shub, Josh Bailis, Debbie Miller, Sidney Korman, Malcomn Shub, Faith Finkelman, Marvin Miller, Joey Miller, Gail Littman, Peter Weiser, Diane Jessel, Sylvia Finkleman, Bruce Gram, Allan Heisler, Hymie Suraski.

214

Young Judaea Northern Region Convention, February 1952 (location uncertain).

representatives in Montreal and in Toronto.

Our parents tried to involve the children in Jewish culture whenever and as much as possible. Thus, Young Judaea had programmes every Sunday morning in the synagogue's upstairs section with the children divided into groups by age. Programmes were developed by the senior leaders in themes of Zionism, Israel, Israeli music and folk dancing, arts and crafts, and sometimes we had speakers or movies. Often they would prepare a Chanukah or Purim play for the community's enjoyment.

The northern towns of Ontario and Quebec formed the northern region of Young Judaea and were comprised of Rouyn–Noranda, Kirkland Lake, Timmins, Sudbury and North Bay. Each year there was an annual convention in another town. The parents of each town were very interested and helpful in planning and assisting for the success of this gathering. I remember my mother making dozens of sandwiches and pastries for the Shabbat luncheon to be held in our home. Such was the involvement of the town's Jewish people

Northern Region Convention, Sudbury, mid-1950s.

216

in furthering the communal feelings and the Jewish spirit of their youngsters.

When the school year ended some of the kids went off to Camp Shalom, Camp Hagshama and Camp Biluim for one or two months. Other kids stayed home, worked, enjoyed summer in the towns and being with their families. In summary, the life of the young people in Noranda and Rouyn could be very busy, and filled with Jewish activities as well as the sports and extracurricular activities involved in a regular school year.

Besides helping to found Young Judaea in Rouyn–Noranda, Jack Korman also helped locate Young Judaea's Camp Shalom in 1948, which was previously known as Silver Birch Lodge (it was near Gravenhurst, Ontario). Sol Mednick from Noranda claims the honour of being the first camper there because, as the first to arrive, he stuck his foot through the gate to become "the first camper to officially set foot on the property." Later, in 1954, Sol worked as the truck driver and office manager for the camp, in charge of buying camp supplies and picking up kosher meat from the Gravenhurst train station.

In 1959, young Kathy Korman penned an appreciation of her time at Camp Shalom. "Last summer when I went to Camp Shalom, I really enjoyed myself. My counsellors were Judy Morner and Ruthie Fried. There were seven kids in my bunk. At Camp Shalom I learned how to swim, use a bow and arrow, and do arts and crafts. Also one of the most exciting events was a boat trip on the *Sagamo*.

"Once, when our bunk was out on a hike, the counsellors forgot the way, and we thought that we were lost and would never be found. Finally, after ten minutes, which really seemed like an hour to us, we found our way back to the camping site. Thank goodness!

"This year at camp, there was a new sports field which was enjoyed by all the campers. Also, everyone agreed that the food was the best.

"I would go to Camp Shalom, and I hope to go next year, because

Northern Region Convention, Timmins, February 1955.

there were so many activities, just what any camper would want; such as hikes, cookouts, and trips out of the camp grounds that any girl or boy my age would enjoy. This was certainly the most exciting holiday I have ever spent."

And here is another colourful slice-of-life description. Young Judaea's newsletter *Kol Hatsafon* of April 1964 reprinted this 1958 entry from Bernadine Miller, which seemed to capture the flavour of some typical experiences for youngsters within Young Judaea: "This year in Young Judaea we have done finger-painting, made little turtles with walnut shells, read stories, played games, and talked about things. We are hoping to have a play ready for the convention. We are planning on sending pictures to Israel of what we do here and in return they will send us pictures of what they do there. We also made place cards for an important banquet. We made puppets. I made one with green hair. I hope this shall be a very successful year since we have new leaders."

One could say that the success of these Young Judaeans could echo the words of Theodore Herzl: "If you will it, it is not a dream." §

Welcome Judaeans! This meeting took place in Rouyn–Noranda. Many
participants were from Rouyn–Noranda (N), with others from Kirkland Lake (K)
and Engelhart (E).

⁂ Front row (left to right): Mr. & Mrs. Goldiner (N), Ruth Fried (N), Sammy
Mallin (K), Vicky Brown (K), unknown, unknown, Irving Brown (K), Norma Miller
(N).

⁂ Middle row (left to right): Sharon Finkelman (K), Stanley Mednick (N),

Judy Miller (N), Adrien Scott (K), Lester Brown (K), Sandra Martin (N), Marvin Wiesenthal (N), Lorne Duke (K), Serena Kokotow (K), Vivian Spiegelman (K), Hariette Kokotow (K), Irving Isenberg (N), Norman Ironstone (N), Eleanor Kokotow (K), Marilyn Ironstone (N), Florence Wiesenthal (N).

ờ Back row (left to right): Goldiner, Mona Garmaise (N), Norman Wiesenthal (N), Bernadine Miller (N), Laurie Miller (N), Beverly Korman (E), Harvey Korman (N), Jerry Korman (N), Kathy Korman (N), Esther Korman (N), David Garmaise (N).

Young Judaea Convention,
Rouyn–Noranda, early 1950s.

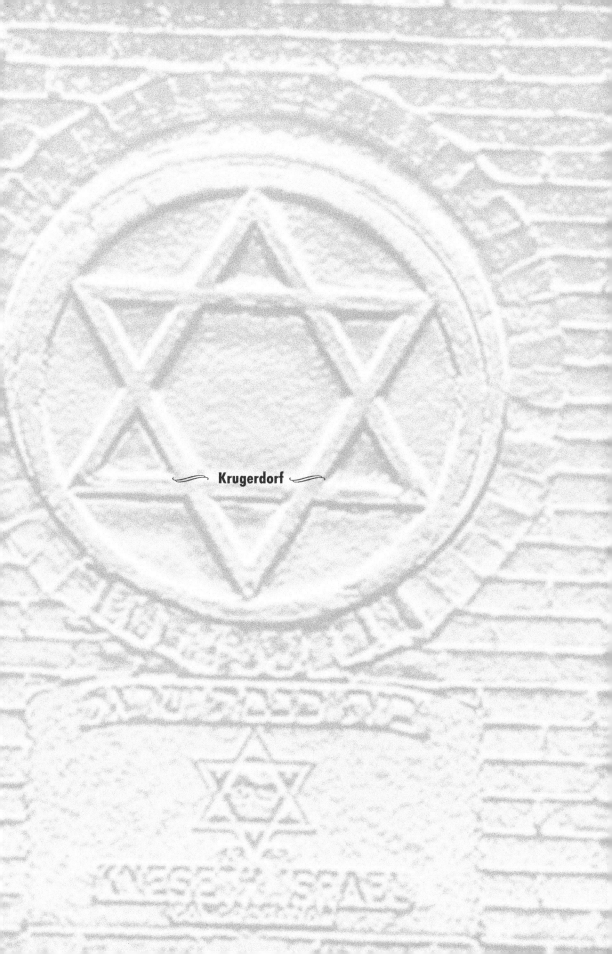

Krugerdorf

Headstone of drowning victim "Ben Tsion ben Nechemia ha-Kohen [Perkus] from Tiraspol, drowned in the river. Kruger's Dorf, N[orthern] Ont[ario]," died June 30, 1908. The stone is obviously not the original. (Photo by Bill Steer)

Krugerdorf — A Remote Northern Jewish Cemetery

Based on research by Bill Steer and Frank Giorno

KRUGERDORF, A JEWISH CEMETERY located between Kirkland Lake and Englehart, Ontario, was founded about 1908 to serve a group of scattered Jewish communities of the North. Towns included Kirkland Lake, Englehart, Iroquois Falls (Ansonville), Cobalt, Haileybury, and Rouyn–Noranda across the Quebec border.

The name Krugerdorf comes from the original German settler, August Kruger, who was given title to 800 acres of land in the late nineteenth century. He established a farm and a blacksmith shop, and helped provide ties and spikes to the Temiskaming and Northern Ontario Railway (later known as the Ontario Northland Railway).

After free land was offered to settlers along the railroad between 1905 and 1915, a group of Jewish settlers from Russia and Romania arrived to establish a small Jewish farming community that had been

Krugerdorf
"chapel"

funded by the Baron de Hirsch Fund. There were about fifty families in all, including Henerofsky, Gurevitch, Feldman, Levy, Goldstein, Abraham, Frumpkin, Verlieb and others.

Originally called the Northern Chevra Kadisha Cemetery, the Jewish burial ground was established when some Jewish pioneers died in a canoeing accident near Tomstown, in Temiskaming region. "Morris Perkus and his son Ben were returning from Englehart station with three new immigrants from Europe when their boat was caught in a surprise current and took them over a waterfall," said historian Henry Abramson, who grew up in Ansonville.

"When the bodies were recovered some time later, they were interred in a section of farmer Simon Henerofsky's property. This property was deeded in 1910 to the Hebrew congregation in Englehart to be used as a cemetery."

In the nearly 120 years since the cemetery was established, more than 100 people were buried there. Abramson recalled attending many funerals at the northern *beit ha'chaim* as a child.

"I remember regular pilgrimages to the Krugerdorf cemetery, which covered an area roughly equivalent to that of a hockey rink. I remember in particular the unveiling of the headstone for my grandmother Polly (Pafke) in 1971 when two dozen or so Jewish people gathered from Cochrane to Timmins in the south to pay respects at

Abe Aidelbaum in Krugerdorf cemetery in 2018. (CJN)

the slightly neglected ancestral burial ground.

"I vaguely remember that the old iron gate was locked, but I found a small footpath so we left the cars on the gravel road and carefully made our way through the brambles in our best clothes. There was a medium-sized shed on the graveyard grounds, and after the unveiling, the last Jews of the north stood around and shared a small meal that consisted primarily of hard-boiled eggs."

Abe Aidelbaum, who died in 2021 at age ninety-three, had been one of the last remaining Jews of Kirkland Lake. As president of the Northern Chevra Kadisha Krugerdorf Cemetery, he had taken upon himself the task of trying to put a funding system in place to replenish the diminishing funds that had been used for Krugerdorf's upkeep.

"Maintenance is a big part of it," he said in an interview in 2018. "The grass needs cutting and trimming around the headstones. The old chapel needs maintaining."

Although some Jewish residents of Rouyn–Noranda were buried at Krugerdorf, most arranged to be buried near their kin in Toronto, Montreal and Ottawa.

It's customary for visitors to a Jewish cemetery to leave a stone on

Fourth Ave & Englehart Post

FRUIT

ICE CREAM

THEN - Fourth Avenue - NOW

Jewish Community Settles Near Englehart

Natives of Ontario were not the only ones attracted by the potential of New Ontario at the turn of the century, and Chamberlain township, close to Englehart became the haven for immigrants who had left Europe because of oppression and attempts to stifle their culture and religion.

Early in the 1900's a benevolent organization known as the "Baron DeHirsh Institute of Montreal" settled a group of Jewish refugees along the north bank of the White River, about eight miles from Englehart.

None of the original colonists remain in the settlement, nor do any of their descendants. Zalek Vertlieb and his sister, were the last to sell their property, moving on to Englehart where they lived for some time before moving to Toronto.

plot on the farm of Simon Henerofsky.

Mr. Henerofsky gave the community a portion of his land to be used as a cemetery for members of the Jewish congregation, and this is still maintained by congregations across Northern Ontario and Northwestern Quebec.

Still living in Englehart is the revered, industrious and affable David Korman, ex-mayor, ex-councillor and businessman, who brought drive and vision to his adopted home which was and is an important factor in the continued growth of the town.

Samuel Henerofsky also moved into the railway centre and contributed to its growth, serving on council and establishing his drug business. Others from the colony who made their mark and became important citizens were Charles Malen, Aaoran Gurevich.

Early in the history of this interesting colony tragedy struck, and three of the immigrants were drowned in the White during a canoe trip. When the bodies were recovered they were buried in a

Classified Ads Bring Results

W. J. HILL, Chairman of the Temis. Centennial Committee, and Hill Secretary-Treasurer and President of the Chamber of Commerce.

the tombstone of their loved ones, but at a remote site like Krugerdorf, which receives relatively few visitors, people sometimes expand upon the custom.

"When I go up with my kids, we like to leave a stone on all of the tombstones, since they get so few visitors," Abramson said. §

Scrapbook

Jewish Congress,
Baron De Hirsh Bldg.,
2040 Bleury St.,
Montreal, Que.

Rouyn Que
Feb 7-34

This letter, dated February 7, 1934, was written on behalf of an ad-hoc Aid Committee in Rouyn–Noranda in response to an appeal from Canadian Jewish Congress. Committee members write that they are sending a money order for $45 to help their Jewish brethren in Germany. They express their sympathy to their brethren and state they are a small shtetl of 25 families. Names of committee members appear at lower right: Yakov Ritter, Sol Miller, Yosef Mednick, Adi [Eddie] Rice. An acknowledgement was received shortly afterwards from H. M. Caiserman, general secretary of Canadian Jewish Congress. [cjcArchives]

די אידישע געמיינדעם אין רוזען און אין נאָראַנדאַ

פֿון ח. מ. קייזערמאן

(איינדרוקעד פון א באזור)

רוען און נאָראַנדאַ זיינען צוויי באַ־
זונדערע שטעדטם מיט צווי שטאָדט־מאַ־
וואַלטונגען. אבער אין דער אמת'ן זיי־
נען זיי איין שטאָדט מיט א געמיינשער
באַפֿעלקערונג פֿון ארום 25 טויזענט
נפשות, באַשטיייענדיג פֿון פֿראַנצויזישע
און ענגלישע קאַנאַדער און אויך סלאַװען
און אַנדערע מינדערייטעטן.

אין רוען און וואוינען פופֿצעהן אידישע
פֿאַמיליעס, און אין נאָראַנדאַ 18 אידי־
שע פֿאַמיליעס. אז אמת
זאגטנע שוחל וועלכע הייסט „כנסת יש־
ראל" און וועלכע קאסט נאַהענט צו 50
טויזענט דאַלאַר, פֿון וועלכער סומע צווי
דרימעל איז שוין [אויסגעצאהלט. דער
פרעזידענט פֿון דער שוחל איז מר. לואיס
 סאַקס. דא וואוינט שוין זיינע יאָהרען

דער אדוואָקאַט מ. דוש. גאָרטייג, וועל־
בער האָט אַלע יאָהרען זיך געועלישאַפֿט־
ליך באַטיילינט אין אַלע אידישע אונ־
טערנעהמונגען, דא וואוינען זעקס מיש־
פחות קאַרלמאַן, צווי משפחות מעזניק,
ה. ר. אייראַנסטאַ, י. מולער, פֿידרי
סאָנדבערג, מאַקס מאַרטין. — אַלע מעג־
שן וועלבע איד גערענק ווען איך בין
דא געוועזן מיט זעקר יאָהרען צוריק און
אַנדערע יונגע ענערגישע אידן.

דער טעמפּא פֿון די צווי שטאָדטלאַ
איז גרוים־ שמאָדטיש, זעהר שעהגע גאָ
סען, שעהגע געשעפֿטען, א גרוים־ע צידר־
קאָלאַציע פֿון אַטאָמאָבילען, טראַנספּאָרט־
קאָמפּאַניען, אַטאַבוסען, אַזוי ווי אין די
גרוים־ע שטעדט — און די אידישע שוחל
איז אויך געבויט געווארדען גרוים־ שטאָ
טיש. — פֿיל גרעסער ווי די איצטיגע נוי־
טען פֿאַדערן עם.

אויסער דער שוחל איז פֿאַרהאַן א
הדסה צווייג. די בני ברית ארגאַניזאַצּיע,
וואס האָט דארטן עקזיסטירט, איז אויפֿ
געגעבען געווארען. א שוחם וועלבער איז
דארט געווען פֿיל יאָהרען, איז געשמאָר־
בען, אזוי אז איצט אין נישטאָ קיין שו־
חט, קיין לעהרער, קיין חזן. עם איז נאָר
פֿאַרהאַן א צאהל איבערגעגעבענע אידן
וועלבע טוען וואס זיי קענען אז מען זאל
ביישטיומיערען. צו די וויכטיגע פֿאַנדערן פֿון
אידישען לעבען. דאָם געבען איז א פֿאַ
שרענקט אויף קלענערע סומען איידער
אין אַנדערע געמיינדעם פֿון זעל'בער צאל
אירען. מיט אַנדערע ווערטער — דאָם
זעל'בע פּראָבלעם ווי אין די אַנדערע גע־
מיינדעם וועלבע איך האַפּ רעהרמאַהנט
אין מיינע צווי פֿריהערדריגע ארטיסלען.

קליינע געמיינדעם ווילען מאַהו זיי'
רע פֿליכטען צו די אידישע נויטען און
פֿאַראַנטזוּוערטליכקייטען — אבער קענען
עם נישט מאַהו גרוים־ שטאָדטיש. זיי
קענען נישט אויפהאַלטען א באַאַמטונג־
טום פֿאַר אידישקייט, און מוזן זיין פֿאַר־
איינינט טראַץ דער פֿאַרשידענקיַט פֿון
די מענטשען וועלבע שטעל'ען צונויף א

קליינע געמיינדע איז בעצאמטען פֿאַ־
דאַרף א קליינע געמיינדע, א געסטיגע
פֿירער, וועל'בער זאל סטימולירען. פֿירען
און מאַקע אַליין אַלע טאַהן און צוגגריי־
טען. ער מוז זיין א חזן כדי צוזאמענצו־
האַלמען די אידען אין שוחל; ער מוז
זיין א לעהרדן און וועל'בער זאל איבעראַצי־
גען יעדעם פֿאַטער פֿאַרשרייבען זיין
קינד אין תלמוד תורה אונ' אַרצישהען;
ער מוז אויך זיין א שוחט. דער אידישער
לעהרער סעמינאר, אויב ער וויל קענען
צושטעל'ען לעהרער צו קליינע געמיינדעם,
מוז זיך רעכגען מים די ספעצישל'ע באַ
דינגונגען אין די דאזיגע געמיינדעם. ער
מוז צוגגריייטען א טיפּ לעהרער וועל'בער
זאל אויך זיין א גיסטין א רעלי'גיעזער
פֿיהרער כרי ער זאל זיך קענען צופאַסען
צו די קליינע געמיינדעם אין זיי סטימו־
לירען.

היינט צו טאָג אין די שוחל א צען־
טער פֿאַר אַלע געמיינדע־ מעטיגקייטען.
אבער עם פעהלט דער גיסטינער אנפיה־
רער און אויפהאלמער. בערות היטלא אַפ
א צאהל פֿאַמיליעס וועלבע ברענגען
פליים פון טאַראַנטאָ.

מיט אזא צופעליגער אידישקייט —
און נאָר ווייניגער אין קלענערע ישבים
— קען מען נישט קומען אין דער צו
קונפֿט מיט אַסטימי'סטישער דערוואַר
טונג סיידען די פֿראָבּלעמען פֿון די קלייני
נע ישבים וועם אויפֿגענומען ווערען פֿון
די נאַצישנאל'ע אידישע קערפערשאפֿטען
מיט ערנסטקייט און מיט אָז אייסגע־
שפּאַרכענעס ווילען די פֿראָבּלעמען צ־
לייזען.

דער פאַקט אז פֿון 33 פֿאַמיליעס וועל'
בע זיינען אייננעל'אַדערן געוואַרען צו א
פֿאַרזאַמל'ונג — און דערמאַהנען נעוואַרען
טעל'עפֿאָניש — זיינען נאָר צעהן געקו־
מען, אז אין אַנדריונג אז דער אינמער
רעם איז נישט קיין גרוימ'ער — אין
דער אינטערעסט מוז „אַנטוויקעלט" וע'
רען.

דער פאַקט ווערט אנערקענט פֿון די
פיהרער פֿון די געמיינדעם. אליין קענען
געמיינדעם זאָרגען פֿאַר די קליינע
רוען, לאַקאל'ע גויטען — און פֿאַר די
אַנטראפֿישע און נאַצישנאל'ע פֿאַנדען
אבער נישט פֿאַר די ערציהעריישע,
לאָמטירל'ע און אפֿילו רעלי'גיעזע גויטען.

The Jewish Communities in Rouyn and in Noranda

from Keneder Odler (The Canadian Eagle), circa 1950s

By Ch. M. Kaiserman

(Impressions of a visit)

Rouyn and Noranda are two separate cities with two separate administrations, but in fact they are one city with a mixed population of around 25,000 souls, composed of French and English Canadians and also Slavic and other minorities.

In Rouyn live fifteen Jewish families and in Noranda eighteen Jewish families. They possess a truly beautiful synagogue which is called "Kneseth Israel" and which cost close to $50,000, of which three-quarters has been paid off. The president of the synagogue is Mr. Louis Scott. For years, the lawyer M. Judge Garmaise has lived here. For all of those years he has taken part in all Jewish enterprises. Here live six Korman families, two Mednick families, H.R. Ironstone, Y. Miller, Sidney Sandberg, Max Martin — all people whom I remember when I was here six years ago.

The pace of the two cities is fast, metropolitan. Very beautiful streets, beautiful stores, a great circulation of automobiles, transport trucks, buses, like in the big cities. And the Jewish synagogue was also built on a grand scale, metropolitan — much bigger than the present day community requires.

Besides the synagogue there is a branch of Hadassah. The B'nai Brith organization which existed there was given up. The ritual slaughterer who was there for many years has died, so that there is now no ritual slaughterer there, no Jewish teacher, no cantor. There is only a group of devoted Jews who do what they can to contribute to the important foundations of Jewish life. Giving is limited to smaller amounts compared to other communities of the same number of Jews. In other words — the same problem as in the other communities that I mentioned in my two earlier articles.

Small communities want to fulfill their obligations to Jewish need and responsibilities — but they cannot fulfill them on a large scale — a metropolitan scale. They cannot support a civil service for Jewish life, and must be united in spite of the differences between people who form a small community. A small community needs one official — an intellectual leader, who will stimulate, lead and indeed be able to do and prepare everything alone. He must be a cantor, in order to keep the Jews in shul organized; he must be a Jewish teacher who should convince every father to register his child in Talmud Torah and educate them; he must also be a ritual slaughterer. The Jewish Teachers Seminary, if it wants to supply Jewish teachers to small communities, must take into account the special circumstances in those communities. It must prepare a type of teacher who will also be an intellectual–religious leader in order to adapt to the small communities and stimulate them.

Nowadays the synagogue is a centre for all community activities. But it is lacking the spiritual leader and supervisor. A number of families who observe *kashruth* bring kosher meat from Toronto.

With such a fortuitous Jewishness — and even less in smaller settlements — one cannot look to the future with optimistic expectations, unless the problems of the small settlements are addressed by the national Jewish associations, with earnestness and with an outspoken will to solve the problems.

The fact that among 33 families who were invited to a meeting — and were reminded by telephone — only 10 came, is an indication that there is not a lot of interest. And interest must be developed.

This fact is becoming recognized by the leaders of the communities. The communities themselves can care for local Jewish needs — and for the philanthropic and national associations — but not for the educational, cultural, and even religious needs. §

Jewish New Year Observed Here

As the sun sank behind the western horizon on Sunday night the Jewish community of Rouyn-Noranda, with quite a number of visitors from Val d'Or, Malartic and other parts, in common with millions of Jews the world over, ushered in the new year 5,708. Rosh Hashanah (the beginning of a new year) was observed in the Noranda synagogue, with a very large attendance at the services, which were conducted by H. Eisenberg, Winnipeg.

Jewish places of business in Rouyn and Noranda were closed on Monday and Tuesday during the observance of the traditional Jewish service which commemorates Rosh Hoshanah, the blowing of the Shofar (ram's horn trumpet), and the reading of the Torah, constitute the official opening of the most sacred of Judaist holidays. Continuing for a period of ten days, it is known as the High Holiday of Ten Bays of Penance and is climaxed by the Day of ——ment, or Yom Kippur.

——mputed according to the an— Jewish lunar calendar which ——sed on revolutions of the —— around the earth, Rosh Has—— has undergone only one ——t variance in observance. In ——days Jews in Palestine relied —— on messages from Jerusalem ——ll them of the advent of the ——ay. Since the length of the ——f worship was determined by ——coming of the new moon, pro—— ——ations from Jerusalem had to ——ent into rural localities ad—— ——g the inhabitants that the —— had come and the day was ——ally over.

——metimes it took many hours ——such proclamations to reach ——eople and more often than not ——holiday continued through ten —— While orthodox Jews still —— the old custom of a two-day ——rvance of Rosh Hashanah, lib— ——Jews have shortened this ——d to twenty-four hours.

——e blowing of the ram's horn ——hofar in ancient days her— ——l a call to battle or a forth— ——ng proclamation. To a mod— ——few it is a challenge to "self— ——ination" . . . a command to ——t his sins and atune himself ——the world and its Maker.

——the eve of Yom Kippur, next ——day, a day of fast begins. ——ces are started which last ——gh the following day and ——purging from sin is com—

Jewish People Observe The New Year Holidays

On Saturday and Sunday last Jewish people of Rouyn-Noranda, in common with Jews throughout the world, celebrated the holy days "Rosh Hashanah", the Jewish New Year, and all Jewish places of business were closed. The observance of the festival had more than usual significance this year following the winning of victory over the Nazis and other forces of aggression against the Jews. The New Year was 5706, and Jewish tradition ascribes the creation of the world on this date. The occasion is one for very solemn observance by the members of the Jewish race and rich in ceremony and religious tradition. Many Jews from out-of-town attended the religious exercises in the Noranda synagogue on Saturday, coming from Beattle, Malartic, Val d'Or-Bourlamaque, Amos, and other centres. With Rev. Mr. Katz, of Rouyn, and Rev. Mr. Eisenberg, of Winnipeg, as cantors, services were held from 8 a.m. to 2.30 p.m. and from 5 to 8 p.m. Next Monday will be another Jewish holiday, for the observance of Yom Kippur.

Jewish Holiday Well Observed

Jewish People Spend Day at Synagogue Following Ritualistic Services

Hope for oppressed mankind extended in the "Atlantic Charter" of Prime Minister Churchill and President Roosevelt was embodied in Isaiah's prophecies many centuries before that declaration of democratic ideals, Vice-President B. Zifkin of Knesseth Israel synagogue, Noranda, declared in an address delivered there on Monday during celebration of the Jewish Day of Atonement (Yom Kippur).

Co-religionists from a wide area in western Quebec joined the local synagogue congregation for the 24-hour observance.

Solemnities began at sunset on Sunday at 7.05 p.m., and continued through to sunset on Monday. All worshippers were in their places continuously except for the hours devoted to sleep and, on Monday, scheduled recess periods.

The ritualistic services were conducted by Rev. M. W. Katz. Other members of the synagogue executive who took official part in the day-long observance were Dr. H. R. Ironstone, president of the synagogue, and Jack Ritter, secretary-treasurer.

Yom Kipper is the most solemn holiday in the Jewish calendar and is strictly observed. For the holiday practically all Jewish professional and business men closed their offices and stores and rigorously followed the religious ritual prescribed for the day.

238

ROUYN-NORANDA PRESS,
QUE. SEPT. 30/43

Jewish People Observe New Year Holidays

Jewish business houses and offices in Rouyn and Noranda are closed to-day and will remain closed to-morrow (Friday) for observance of Rosh Hashanah, the Jewish New Year, which commenced at sundown last evening. In Noranda synagogue services were held last evening and to-day and will continue to-morrow, with co-religionists from different parts of this region joining in the exercises, which are being conducted by Rev. M. W. Katz. All Jewish business places are closed during the two days of the New Year and on the Day of Atonement, which will occur this year on Saturday, Oct. 9, while Jewish school children remain absent from their classes in order to participate in the services. There are also observances in the homes, and quite a number of local people have gone to join their families in other places for the holiday period.

New Russell Syn. Synagogue

ROUYN-NORANDA PRESS
P. Q., OCT. 27/49

New Synagogue Officially Opened Following Parade Last Sunday

Michael Korman, president of the local Jewish Community, cut the ribbon to officially open the New Kneseth Israel Synagogue on Ninth Street in Noranda last Sunday afternoon. The short opening ceremony followed a parade of the Jewish Community led by the Canadian Corps Band from the home of Joseph Korman on Third Avenue.

Joseph Korman cut the ribbon on the inner door to open the main part of the building. In the procession Mr. Korman carried the scrolls of the Torah which he and Mrs. Korman and their son had presented to the synagogue. A religious service was held commemorating the official opening.

A dinner and dance was held in the hall in the evening to mark the happy occasion for the local Jewish community. Dr. Harry Ironstone presided at the dinner and welcomed the out of town guests. In his opening remarks he recalled that Mr. and Mrs. D. Caplan were the first Jewish people to come to the twin cities, and that they were followed by Mr. and Mrs. I. Rice, Mr. and Mrs. Louis Scott, Mr. and Mrs. Sidney Sandberg and Mr. and Mrs. Mike Korman.

Praise was given to the work of Michael Korman who had given so much of his time to see that the new building was built. He was presented following the dinner with a gold watch by Nathan Weisenthal on behalf of the Jewish community. Wallets were also presented to B. Zifkin and Charles Steinberg in appreciation of their work.

Among the speakers were Joseph Korman, I. Rice, of the building committee, Mrs. Louis Scott, president of the Ladies Hadassah; Louis Revzen, president of B'Nai B'rith; Sam Davis, Kirkland Lake, Jack Ritter, M. Sharony, Frank Conlon, editor of the Rouyn-Noranda Press; and others.

Following the dinner dancing was enjoyed to the music of Harry Byzick and his orchestra.

ROUYN-NORANDA PRESS, QUE.
NOV. 5/42

Hebrew Congregation Is Now Incorporated

Notice appeared in the last issue of the Quebec Official Gazette that letters patent have been issued to incorporate as a corporation without share capital Dr. Harry Raymond Ironstone, dentist, Benjamin Zifkin, photographer, both of the town of Noranda, and Jack Ritter, merchant, of the town of Rouyn, province of Quebec, for the following purposes: To be constituted into an organization, its principal objects being to promote the advancement of religion among the Hebrew residents of Rouyn and Noranda and surroundings, to conduct religious services in a suitable synagogue, to extend charity to persons professing the Hebrew or other faiths, and to encourage social and cultural activities among its members; but without pecuniary gain, under the name of "Rouyn-Noranda Hebrew Congregation." The amount to which the value of the immoveable property which the corporation may hold is to be limited, is twenty thousand dollars ($20,000.) The head office of the corporation will be at Noranda.

New Kneseth Israel

NORTHERN DAILY NEWS
KIRKLAND LAKE ONT
OCT. 24/49

New Synagogue Opened At Noranda

NORANDA, Que.—(Staff Special) —The New Kneseth Israel Synagogue, Ninth street, Noranda, was officially opened at 6.30 p.m. yesterday.

Earlier in the afternoon, a Torah was presented to the Synagogue by Mr. and Mrs. Joseph Korman, and the corner stone was unveiled by the president, Michael Korman.

Finished last year, the building was constructed and finished through the contributions of the Jewish population of the twin cities and neighboring communities.

Synagogue

New Kneseth

The New Synagogue

LAST SUNDAY WITH IMPRESSIVE ceremonies the New Kneseth Israel Synagogue in Noranda was officially opened and dedicated to the services of God.

The members of the Jewish Community are to be congratulated on their achievement. The approximately thirty Jewish families in the twin cities at great sacrifices to each of them have erected a synagogue that is a credit to them and a fitting place to carry on their worship.

The Press unites with the non-Jewish members of our community in congratulating our Jewish friends on their achievement and extends to them best wishes for their future in their new religious home.

...for three weeks, and returned home Sept. 12th.

The Jewish community of Rouyn-Noranda and outlying towns began the observance of the New Year of 5707 at sunset last evening. Tomorrow (Friday) is New Year's Day, and the observance of this feast is being conducted with services at the Synagogue by Rev. W. M. Katz throughout today and tomorrow. They are being well attended by local residents and visitors, and all Jewish places of business are closed until Saturday morning.

Miss Carol MacLachlan, of Noranda, left on T...

Solemn Week In Jewish Life

New Years and Yom Kippur Important Holydays Held In October

A solemn period in the religious life of Jewish people all over the world begins this week-end. The local Jewish community will observe the holy days in the new synagogue, now nearing completion on Ninth street. Beginning Sunday at sundown and continuing until sundown Tuesday evening, the period is known as Rosh Hashanah, New Year's. The feast inaugurates ten days of penitence, the most solemn in the Jewish calendar, which have been set aside for retrospection and self-examination. Cantor Harry Eisenberg, of Winnipeg, will be in charge of the services for Rosh Hashanah which are followed by Yom Kippur on October 13th.

Reverend J. H. Diamond, of Noranda, will perform the ancient and involved ritual of the blowing of the Shofar, the ram's horn, reminding the Jewish people of the need for self-examination. Many visitors from out of town are expected to attend the services here.

Before and during the ten days of penitence is the period when Jewish people exchange New Year

Yom Kippur Is Great Holyday

Twin Cities' Jewish Community And Visitors Attend Synagogue

The Jewish community of Rouyn-Noranda, with many out-of-town visitors, joined their brethren from all over the world on Tuesday evening, at sun-down, for the start of the great annual holy day of the year Yom Kippur, or as it is known in English, The Day of Atonement. Services were conducted by H. Eisenberg, of Winnipeg. As the name signifies, it was a day of meditation and prayer for members of the Hebrew faith. A day in which repentance for their sins was made in spiritual exercises. From sun-down Tuesday until after sun-down Wednesday Jewish people the world over fasted and abstained from food and drink as mortification and penance.

Jewish places of business in the twin cities traditionally are closed on this the greatest day of the year. Visitors from Malartic, Val d'Or, Duparquet, Cobalt and other places again came to the little frame synagogue on Eighth St., Noranda for the services, which continued throughout the whole of the day.

Yom Kippur followed by a week, the ushering in of the New Year, Rosh Hashanah, the beginning of the year 5,708, computed according to the ancient Jewish calendar. This is based on the lunar system, and calculated according to revolutions of the moon around the earth.

Mr. Sharony getting a gold medal for leading the Congregation and being the
Hebrew school teacher in Rouyn–Noranda. Toronto, 1988. Left to right: Doreen
Korman, Jerry Korman, Sol Mednick, unknown, Meyer Sharony, Saul Korman.

All smiles for this group photo, taken in Toronto in 1988. From left: Chaskel (Harry)
Korman, Sol Mednick, Ed Mednick, Jerry Korman, Stanley Rice, Mike (Motel)
Smith, Manny Crotin, Saul Korman, Morris Langer, Irving Feldman.

Goldie & I.J. Miller Family.
Boys photo, 1929. Back row: I.J., Harry, Ben. Front row: Morris.
Girls photo, 1944. Left to right: Rose (Korman), Tillie (Cohen),
Arlene (Wise).

Left to right: Lou Revzen, Nelly
Revzen, Isaac Korman, Rose (Miller)
Korman. Circa 1950.

Jewish Marriages in Rouyn–Noranda

All marriages took place in Kneseth Israel Synagogue unless otherwise noted. This list was compiled from known sources and may not be complete.

March 19, 1933	Henry Walter Crotin & Sarah Korman
November 27, 1933	Jack Ritter & Rebecca Erlichman
October 7, 1934	Samuel Davis & Esther Mirrel Korman
October 22, 1937	David Caplan & Luba Garesef Spitzberg
July 30, 1939	Coleman Harry Kleiman & Molly Gordon
March 30, 1941	Morton Cartman & Lily Korman
August 10, 1941	Joseph Korman & Regina Sumak
July 22, 1945	Isaac Korman & Rose Miller (in Noranda Theatre)
August 26, 1945	Edward Weinstein & Helen-Fanny Korman
November 24, 1946	Samuel Korman & Ethel Abel
July 30, 1950	Maury Bloch & Delores Mednick
August 19, 1951	Abraham Deuitch & Pearl Fried
February 24, 1952	Danny Deuitch & Dorothy Mednick
June 15, 1953	Ted Wise & Arlene Miller
June 10, 1962	Harold Perlman & Judy Miller

Rouyn–Noranda winter scene.

ROUYN TELEPHONE DIRECTORY

RING OFF ALWAYS—The Telephone Service would be quickened considerably if Subscribers would Ring Off Always

Amulet Mine	413
Area Mine	411
Banque Canadienne Nationale, Noranda St.	14
Box & Huchnergard, Men's Outfitters, Perrault St.	3
Brundige & Ferguson, Grocers, Rue Blake	4
Burke, O. R., Res. Rue Perrault	22
Canadian Bank Commerce, Perrault St.	31
Corrigan Contracting Syndicate, Rue Begin	23
Dean, J. E., Res. Perrault St.	41
Doyle, Fred, Perrault St.	32
Duprat Mine	417
Duval, Paul, Res.	45
Fortin, Joachim, Contractor, Rouyn	36
Glengarry Cafe, Rue Blake, W. Noice, Prop.	21
Goldfields Hotel, Mrs. F. Wilson, Prop.	15
Horne Copper Corporation	10
Kar, Lém, Cafe, Perrault St.	47
Lafortune & Gagne, Wholesale Merchants, Lake Shore Rd.	11
Laporte, J. L., Contractor, Rue Perrault	19
Laporte, J. R., General Store, Lake Shore Rd.	8
Laval-Quebec Mines, Ltd.	40
Linklater, Dr. E. W., Druggist, Perrault St.	42
Linklater, Dr. E. W., Physician, Noranda Mine	29
Mars Hotel, P. J. Kutianinen, Prop., Noranda St.	20
Nadou & Gamache, Butchers, Lake Shore Rd.	9
Nickle Range Hotel, M. A. Cybulka, Prop.	25
Noice, A. E., Druggist, Rue Blake	26
Noranda Mines (Horne Copper Corporation)	10
Osisko Hotel, J. Green, Prop., Rue Blake	13
Pelletier, Rev. Father, Rue Perrault	1
Pinder, Nelson, Townsite Agent, Rue Perrault	2
Potter, R. S., Contractor & Builder, Rue Taschereau	30
Regal Theatre, H. S. & C. S. Carey, Prop., Rue Perrault	17
Rouyn Hardware, McManus & Johnston, Prop., Rue Perrault	7
Royal Bank of Canada, Rue Perrault	12
Rudd, Dr. M. S., Physician, Rue Perrault	5
Rudd, Dr. M. S., Res.	28
Tattlebaum, M., Ladies' & Gent's Furnishings, Perrault St.	33
Waite-Montgomery Mines	415
Windsor Hotel, E. Dallaire, Prop., Main Ave.	16

SPEAKER PRINT

Rouyn–Noranda's first telephone directory, issued 1926.

EDDIE'S BOWLING LANES ROUYN

PHOTO BOLDUC

Snow-going vehicle of the Noranda Bread Company, delivering bread across the ice.

F. W. Woolworth Store

Recreation Centre

Mr. and Mrs. Sam Korman Cele - brate Son Harvey's Bar Mitzvah

Mr. and Mrs. Sam Korman of Noranda fulfilled a special wish when they celebrated the Bar Mitzvah of their oldest son Harvey. Mr. Korman is a well known theatre and real estate man of the twin cities.

175 guests attended the Saturday evening cocktail and banquet at the Noranda Hotel.

The religious ceremony was held Saturday morning at Knesseth Israel Congregation. After the ceremony a luncheon was held at the Elizabeth Room of the Windsor Hotel. Friday evening, the family and close friends celebrated at the home of Mr. and Mrs. Sam Korman.

Saturday evening, beginning at 7.00 p.m. some 175 friends and relatives gathered to honour the Bar Mitzvah of Harvey Philip Korman. Cocktails were served in the lobby of the Noranda Hotel and was followed by a dinner. Fro the occasion, the Noranda Hotel had the dining room, the Normandy Room and bart of the lobby ready to accomodate the large crowd. A beautiful Bar - Mitzvah cake decorated the head table. It was decorated with lights and adorned with religious symbols including skull caps and the Ten Commandments.

The party was one of the largest individual one of its kind to be held in Noranda.

Guests from as far as California attended. The Noranda Hotel and staff did a grand job of serving a fine dinner to the large attendance.

Attending the Bar - Mitzvah were: Mr. and Mrs. Fredrick Hebert, Mayor of Noranda, Mr. & Mrs. J. Amor, Dr. & Mrs. Juteau, Mr. & Mrs. Bashaw, Mr. & Mrs. A. Fortin, Mr. & Mrs. M. Overchuck, Mr. Portelance, Mr. & Mrs. S. Fried, Mr. & Mrs. V Finkleman & family, Mr. Katz, Mr. & Mrs. H. Iron-

stone, Mr. & Mrs. M. Korman, Mr. & Mrs. I. Korman, & family, Mr. & Mrs. S. Kravetz, & family, Mr. & Mrs. L. Scott & family, Mr. & Mrs. M. Garmaise & family, Mr. & Mrs. Wiesenthal & family, Mr. Terry Shaw, Mr. & Mrs. Ted Soucie, Mr. G. Ort, Mr. & Mrs. Sarsfield, Miss D. Poulin, Mr. & Mrs. J. Ansara

(Continued on Page 2)

Mr. & Mrs. B. Robertson, Mr. & Mrs. T. Bosada, Mrs. Edwards, Mr. & Mrs. P. Lavignis, Mr. & Mrs. W. Krancevic, Mrs. Martino & Son, Mrs. Kitty, Mrs. Miller, Mr. & Mrs. B. Miller & family, Mr. & Mrs. H. Miller & family, Mr. & Mrs. M. Martin & daughter, Mr. & Mrs. E. Rice, Mr. Sharony, California: Mr. & Mrs. C. Horowitz, and Mrs. Horowitz. Israel: Mr. & Mrs. S. Korman. Toronto: Mr. & Mrs. D. Korman, Mr. & Mrs. N. Korman,

Miss Sandberg, Mr. & Mrs. L. Davidson, Miss Doufman, Eddie Mednick, Mr. A. Isenberg, Mr. & Mrs. A. Martin, and Mr. M. Smith. Montreal: Mr. & Mrs. M. Gaison, Mr. & Mrs. A. Levy and family, and Mr. & Mrs. H. Korman. Detroit: Mrs. N. Kling, Mrs. E. Kahn, Mr. & Mrs. M. Black and Mr. S. Korman. Val d'Or: Mrs. A.J. Korman, and Mr. & Mrs. M. Cartman, and family. Ansonville: Mr. Croton & family, and Mr. &

Mrs. W. Croton. Sault St. Marie: Mr. I. Bregman. Sudbury: Mr. & Mrs. D. Field. Kirkland Lake: Mr. Esther Davis, Mr. & Mrs. C. Caplan, Mr. & Mrs. T. Mallin, & Mrs. A. Kokotow, Mr. & Mrs. H. Atkins & son, Mr. & Mrs. J. Dash, & family. North Bay: Mr. & Mrs. E. Wrenstien and family. Galt: Mrs. Shinehoft. St. Catherines: Mr. & Mrs. H. Brandes & family. Timmins: Mr. Alramson and family, and Mr. I. arman.

Guest list from Harvey Korman's bar-mitzvah, as printed in a Rouyn–Noranda newspaper, 1961.

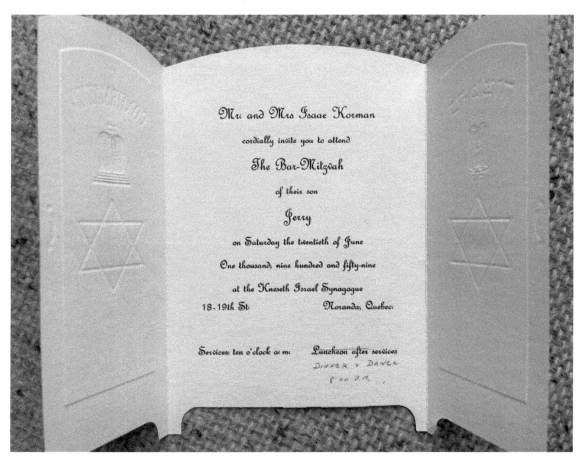

Invitation to Jerry Korman's bar-mitzvah, 1959.

Index
(major references only)

Printed in the USA
CPSIA information can be obtained
at www.ICGtesting.com
LVHW070905280823
756454LV00015B/81